109TH CONGRESS
1ST SESSION

H. R. 235

To amend the Internal Revenue Code of 1986 to protect the religious free
exercise and free speech rights of churches and other houses of worship.

IN THE HOUSE OF REPRESENTATIVES

JANUARY 4, 2005

Mr. JONES of North Carolina introduced the following bill; which was referred
to the Committee on Ways and Means

A BILL

To amend the Internal Revenue Code of 1986 to protect
the religious free exercise and free speech rights of
churches and other houses of worship.

1   *Be it enacted by the Senate and House of Representa-*

2 *tives of the United States of America in Congress assembled,*

3 **SECTION 1. SHORT TITLE.**

4   This Act may be cited as the "Houses of Worship

5 Free Speech Restoration Act of 2005".

6 **SEC. 2. HOUSES OF WORSHIP PERMITTED TO ENGAGE IN**

7   **RELIGIOUS   FREE   EXERCISE   AND   FREE**

8   **SPEECH ACTIVITIES, ETC.**

9   (a) IN GENERAL.—Section 501 of the Internal Rev-

10 enue Code of 1986 is amended by redesignating subsection

1 (q) as subsection (r) and by inserting after subsection (p)

2 the following new subsection:

3 "(q) An organization described in section

4 170(b)(1)(a)(1) or section 508(c)(1)(A) shall not fail to

5 be treated as organized and operated exclusively for a reli-

6 gious purpose, nor shall it be deemed to have participated

7 in, or intervened in any political campaign on behalf of

8 (or in opposition to) any candidate for public office, for

9 purposes of subsection (c)(3) or section 170(c)(2), 2055,

10 2106, 2522, or 4955 because of the content, preparation,

11 or presentation of any homily, sermon, teaching, dialectic,

12 or other presentation made during religious services or

13 gatherings.".

14   (b) EFFECTIVE DATE.—The amendment made by

15 subsection (a) shall apply to taxable years ending after

16 the date of enactment of this Act.

17 SEC. 3. CAMPAIGN FINANCE LAWS UNAFFECTED.

18   No member or leader of an organization described in

19 section 501(q) of the Internal Revenue Code of 1986 (as

20 added by section 2) shall be prohibited from expressing

21 personal views on political matters or elections for public

22 office during regular religious services, so long as these

23 views are not disseminated beyond the members and

24 guests assembled together at the service. For purposes of

25 the preceding sentence, dissemination beyond the members

1 and guests assembled together at a service includes a mail-
2 ing that results in more than an incremental cost to the
3 organization and any electioneering communication under
4 section 304(f) of the Federal Election Campaign Act of
5 1971 (2 U.S.C. 434(f)). Nothing in the amendment made
6 by section 2 shall be construed to permit any disburse-
7 ments for electioneering communications or political ex-
8 penditures prohibited by the Federal Election Campaign
9 Act of 1971.

○

FOREWORD BY D. JAMES KENNEDY

Introduction by Congressman Walter B. Jones

GAG ORDER

How An Unjust Law Is Being Used To Silence Pastors

Compiled and edited by

GARY CASS

EXECUTIVE DIRECTOR, CENTER TO RECLAIM AMERICA

The D. James Kennedy
CENTER for
RECLAIMING AMERICA

Gag Order
by Coral Ridge Ministries
Compiled ane edited by Dr. Gary Cass

Printed in the United States of America

ISBN 1-594679-84-3

Center for Reclaiming America
P.O. Box 632
Ft. Lauderdale, FL 33302
877-SALT-USA (725-8872)
www.ReclaimAmerica.org

Xulon Press
10640 Main Street
Suite 800
Fairfax, VA 22030
(703) 279-6511
www.xulonpress.com

Table of Contents

Dedication and Acknowledgements

This book would not have been possible without the dedicated staff at Xulon Press, Inc. Also special thanks to John Amon and Sam Kastensmidt of Coral Ridge Ministries for their research assistance, Sam A. Jernigan IV of Congressman Jones' office for coordination, and Dr. D. James Kennedy for indefatigable inspiration and courage. This book is dedicated to pastors and other church leaders who are boldly proclaiming the truth in the face of persecution and prosecution.

A Time for Freedom

By Dr. D. James Kennedy

A merican culture has been under withering attack for over a generation. So much so that the virtues that built Western Civilization are giving way in some quarters to paganism. How else to describe the open defense of infanticide in the U.S. Supreme Court's ruling upholding partial-birth abortion as a right under the Constitution, or the 2003 ruling from the Massachusetts high court that same-sex marriage is protected under the state constitution.

In the face of all this, the clergy of America are far too silent. Why? For some, a theology that places "political" questions outside the purview of the pulpit has served as an effective muzzle. For others, the fear of congregational dissent should a controversial topic such as abortion be addressed makes many go mute. Others, misinformed about the true meaning of the First Amendment, may think it somehow unconstitutional to address the public square from within the four walls of a church.

But all clergy, regardless of their theology or personal "fear factor" are concerned that the Internal Revenue Service will launch an expensive and time-consuming investigation if they even come close to committing what the IRS has loosely defined as "political activity."

The silence of the clergy today is entirely at odds with American history—indeed with the Western legal tradition. It was, after all, Stephen Langton, the Archbishop of Canterbury who in 1215 sided with the barons in their dispute with King John and drafted Magna Carta, a document which has been called "the foundation on which has come to rest the entire structure of Anglo-American constitutional liberties." [Richard L. Perry, Editor, Sources of Our Liberties (Chicago: American Bar Foundation, 1978), p. 1]. Magna Carta established the rule of law in place of the arbitrary, tyrannical rule of princes. Archbishop Langton did not remain silent.

In America, clergyman John Witherspoon signed the Declaration of Independence and, as president of the College of New Jersey (later Princeton College), influenced a generation of American statesmen, including James Madison. Under Witherspoon's leadership, the Presbyterian school for training ministers came to be called by the British a "seminary of sedition."

Witherspoon told his students: "It is in the man of piety and inward principle, that we may expect to find the uncorrupted patriot, the useful citizen, and the invincible soldier. God grant that in America true religion and civil liberty may be inseparable." John Witherspoon did not remain silent.

Nor did Jonas Clark. A pastor in Lexington, Massachusetts, he was the most influential churchman and politician in the Lexington-Concord region at the time of the Revolutionary War, according to Franklin Cole, editor of They Preached Liberty.

On April 18, 1775, he entertained John Hancock and Samuel Adams at his home. These two great patriots asked him, "If war came, would the people of Lexington fight?" He is said to have replied, "I have trained them for this very hour."

The next day the "shot heard round the world" was fired on his church lawn as the British drew first blood in the opening battle of the Revolutionary War. Eight men were killed, all members of Rev. Clark's congregation. As he looked down, in great anguish, at the bodies of those who had fallen, he said, "From this day will be dated the liberty of the world."

It began in a church. It began with a parson who was not afraid to speak out on the great issues of freedom, liberty, oppression, and tyranny. (One of Rev. Clark's most notable printed sermons: "The Fate of Blood-Thirsty Oppressors.")

Rev. Clark was a part of the "Black Regiment," Revolutionary patriot-preachers who, in their black robes, preached fiery sermons about the evils of tyranny and set the stage for liberty in America—a liberty which, as Clark predicted, has spread to many other nations across the world.

Today, however, too few preachers are willing to raise their voice on contemporary moral issues. And, of course, federal tax law offers a justification to remain silent.

Fortunately, there is something we can do to remove the legal restraint on the clergy of America. Gag Order, edited by Dr. Gary Cass, illuminates this issue as few other works have done. I recommend it to your careful reading and consideration. It is my prayer that it will prompt you to urge your elected representatives to repeal the 1954 "gag order" that has so effectively silenced so many in the Church.

In a culture like ours, which sometimes seems on moral life support, the voice of the Church and her message of reconciliation, virtue, and hope is more important now than ever before. Yet the current law has effectively silenced the Church. We are a poorer nation for it.

The free speech rights of America's clergy have been

improperly denied for much too long. It is time to return to the historical role of the pulpit. It is time to restore true freedom of speech to America's houses of worship.

—D. James Kennedy, Ph.D.

Introduction

By Congressman Walter B. Jones Jr.

A s an American, I believe that the greatest gift imparted to our nation at the hands of a gracious Father is that enshrined in the First Amendment to the Constitution. Our forefathers in their inspired wisdom chose the sanctity of free speech and the free exercise of religion as the first and most supreme of all protections when crafting the Bill of Rights. America, a nation conceived and founded upon the most solemn of Judeo-Christian tenets stands at a moment of inflection. Our moral resolve and commitment to the principles that have made this society a "shining city upon a hill" stand challenged, and I fear extinguished. Since 1995, when I first entered Congress, I have looked for and sought to foster issues and causes that serve to reconstitute the moral and spiritual authority of our country. Like many of you, I have been disheartened and at times shocked by the seemingly constant assault on America's "moral voice." To prevent the extreme left and secularists who would seek to tear apart the spiritual fabric underpinning our society I have campaigned for and made it my mission to rectify an injustice of the past and reignite the passion and fire of our religious leaders.

H.R. 235 - *The Houses of Worship Free Speech*

Restoration Act of 2005 is legislation that will finally remove the muzzle from our pastors, priests, rabbis, and clerics and return freedom of speech to the pulpit. From the days of the Constitutional Convention to 1954 their was never any restriction on freedom of speech in America's houses of worship. I believe with all my heart that to ensure America's future we must embrace the Judeo-Christian mores upon which our country was founded. **H.R. 235** will re-empower our religious leaders to speak out on social, moral, and political issues. Abortion, marriage, social justice, and the very definition and treatment of life are and will continue to be the most controversial and pivotal political issues facing America. More than at any moment in recent history, our moral foundations are being debated in the marketplace of ideas and decided upon by our elected leaders. This backdrop of national discussion and consequence demands our involvement as Christians and the vigilance of all Americans who concede the imperfections of man and the existence of a higher power. With a clergy free of intimidation and oppression, America stands to rediscover the moral compass that made this society the envy of all others.

I feel so blessed and grateful for the many amazing individuals across the country who over the past four years have given their time and unwavering support for this legislation. Seeing the many ways God has been apart of the effort to pass **H.R. 235** has been a truly humbling experience. I pray that this book will only bolster the already incredible momentum of the last few years and with your help, we will pass the language in **H.R. 235** and once and for all return freedom of speech to the pulpits of *every* house of worship in America.

Walter B. Jones Jr.
Member of Congress

CHAPTER ONE

The Glorious Heritage of the American Pulpit

A simple reading of the sermons that surrounded our founding would disabuse anyone of the notion that the church was silent about politics. John Wingate Thornton concluded in 1860 that "in a very great degree, to the pulpit, the PURITAN Pulpit, we owe the moral force which won our independence" (John Wingate Thornton, *The Pulpit of the American Revolution* (Boston: Gould and Lincoln, 1860; reprint, New York: Da Capo, 1970), p. xxxviii).

In fact, if you were part of the "men's fellowship group" in colonial times, your pastor might just end up being your commanding officer in the armed struggle against the British. This makes our Promise Keepers meeting look very tame by comparison! The clergy were often derisively called the "Black Regiment" by the British due to the color of their clerical robes. The clergy and their fiery sermons played a very prominent role in stirring the colonies to throw off the arbitrary and abusive rule of that tyrant, King George.

Sermons fueled the debate and the souls with the

heralding forth of prophetic blood-stirring diatribes. At great personal risk, the Rev. Jacob Cushing preached and published one of the most famous political sermons of the day. It was distributed far and wide.

"Divine Judgements upon Tyrants: And Compassion to the Oppressed."
A SERMON, PREACHED AT LEXINGTON, APRIL 20th, 1778.

In commemoration of the MURDEROUS WAR and Rapine, inhumanely perpetrated, by two brigades of British troops, in that town and neighbourhood, on the NINETEENTH of APRIL, 1775.

By JACOB CUSHING, A.M., PASTOR of the CHURCH in WALTHAM.

"According to their deeds, accordingly he will repay, fury to his adversaries, recompence to his enemies."
Isaiah lix. 18.

"Say to them that are of a fearful heart, be strong, fear not; behold! your God will come with vengeance, even with a recompence he will come and save you."
Isaiah xxxv. 4

MASSACHUSETTS-STATE; BOSTON: PRINTED BY POWARS AND WILLIS.
M, DCC, XXVIII

This type of prophetic preaching is not often heard in America. In fact, most seminaries never touch on the great role that the Protestant pulpit in America played in securing our liberty.

Politicians loyal to Britain certainly understood the powerful political influence of these fearless men of God. The governor of Massachusetts complained that pulpits were "filled with such dark covered expressions and the people are led to think they may lawfully resist the King's troops as any foreign enemy" (Alice M. Baldwin, *The New England Clergy and the American Revolution* (Durham: Duke University Press, 1928), p. 113; quoted in Marvin Olasky, *Fighting for Liberty and Virtue* (Wheaton, Illinois: Crossway Books), p. 26; online at http://www.olasky.com/ Archives/liberty/15.pdf).

Preachers had the tack of asserting that the Founders did have Christian grounds for replacing the tyrannical rule of King George. After a long train of abuses and repeated attempts to petition the king for a redress of grievances, the Colonists had been ignored, rebuffed, and mistreated. The king had forfeited his right to rule by abusing his office, and now a government for the people had to be established. "The American Revolution was more than a contest with England. It was a war of ideas, a contest for the hearts and minds of men. It was a war to defend a vision about law, rights, justice, and the God-given dignity of men" (Gary Amos, *Defending the Declaration,* Brentwood, Wolgemuth & Hyatt Pub. Inc., p. 169). These great principles and noble ideals were the fruit of centuries of Christian law theory rooted in the Bible. Thank God for wise, well-read, and courageous ministers of Christ.

Prime Minister Horace Walpole declared in Parliament the source of much of their problems across the Atlantic. "Cousin America has run off with a Presbyterian parson." He was likely referring to John Witherspoon, a Presbyterian minister, president of Princeton and a signer of the Declaration of Independence. Witherspoon was accused of turning his college into a "seminary of sedition." No doubt he was the most important "political parson" of the Revolutionary period, according to the Library of Congress. He was so persuasive that a British officer called him a "political firebrand, who perhaps had not a less share in the Revolution than Washington himself. He poisons the minds of his young students and through them the Continent" (Varnum Lansing Collins, *President Witherspoon* (New York: Arno Press, 1969), p. 133; quoted in Olasky, *Fighting for Liberty and Virtue*, p. 29; online at http://www.olasky. com/Archives/liberty/15.pdf).

The graduates of Yale and Harvard, then serving in churches across New England, laid out the theology of resistance that made war with Britain inevitable. "The ideology for revolution had been expounded for 150 years in New England's pulpits" (Ben Hart, *Faith and Freedom: The Christian Roots of American Liberty* (San Bernardino, California: Here's Life Publishers), p. 227). Back then, the pulpit was the unchallenged central means of public communication. The sermon was so powerful in shaping the culture "that even television pales in comparison" (Harry S. Stout, *The New England Soul: Preaching and Religious Culture in Colonial New England,* New York, 1986, p. 3).

Another of the most provocative and influential sermons preached during the Revolutionary era was Jonathan Mayhew's 1750 "Discourse Concerning Unlimited Submission and Non-Resistance to the Higher Powers." His message, quickly printed and read on both sides of the Atlantic, justified political and military resistance to tyrants and has been called "The Morning Gun of the American Revolution."

Then, as now, critics argued that ministers were remiss in bringing politics into the pulpit. "There are special times and seasons when [the minister] may treat of politics," William Gordon declared in a sermon preached December 15, 1776, in defiance of British General Thomas Gage's prohibition. To that, a loyalist complained: "I most heartily wish, for the peace of America, that he and many others of his profession would confine themselves to gospel truths!"

But for New England's ministers, who had been faithfully applying God's Word to every area of life since the first generation arrived in Massachusetts, "they would be remiss if, as God's watchmen, they failed to sound the alarm" (Stout, *The New England Soul*, p. 284).

The clergy of New England mobilized their flock for war against Britain and stood with them when the "shot heard round the world" rang out. The Rev. Jonas Clark was the most influential churchman and politician in the Lexington-Concord region at the time of the Revolutionary War. On the night of April 18, 1775, Rev. Clark hosted John Hancock and Samuel Adams at his home. When the warning came that evening from Paul Revere that Gen. Gage's soldiers were advancing on Lexington, Clark's guests asked whether the men of his town would fight. He is said to have replied, "I have trained them for this very hour." The pleadings and prayers of all the colonies had no effect on the hardened heart of King George. Now the struggle for liberty would have to be an armed struggle. The next day hostilities erupted, and eight American patriots fell dead on Lexington green.

After Lexington, the British marched on to Concord, where the militia rushed to the village. The first man there was Concord's 32-year-old minister William Emerson. In a sermon he preached a month earlier, Emerson told the militia, "Should we neglect to defend ourselves by military preparation, we never could answer it to God and to our own Consciences or the rising [generations]" (Harry S. Stout, "How Preachers Incited Revolution, *Christian History*, Spring 1996, online article at http://www.christianitytoday. com/holidays/fourthofjuly/features/50h010.html). Aware that the Redcoats might launch a surprise attack, Emerson engaged in a "nonstop pulpit campaign to prepare the towns surrounding Boston for war" (Stout, *The New England Soul*, p. 290). "The rhetoric of the Revolutionary war was often political, but its passions were religious" (David R. Williams, *Revolutionary War Sermons*, Delmar, N.Y.: Scholars Facsimilies and Reprints, 1984, p. xxxiv). During the period of 1740 to 1800, there were over eighteen hundred political sermons preached, and this was just counting two states, Massachusetts and Connecticut (Ibid., p. x).

In 1860, Thorton concluded that "the true alliance between Politics and Religion is the lesson in this volume of sermons ... it is the voice of the Fathers of the Republic, enforced by their example. They invoked God in their civil assemblies, called upon their chosen teachers of religions to counsel from the Bible, and recognized it precepts as the law of their public conduct. The Fathers did not divorce politics and religion, but they denounced the separation as ungodly" (Thorton, op.cit., p. i).

After the Revolutionary War, the clergy did not retreat to the ivory towers of abstract speculation, nor into a theology of isolationism from a fallen world. Research has shown that for a century after the Revolutionary War, the pulpits were among the most influential aspects of political life in America. It was the message of the Bible that created the political self-consciousness of most Americans. The Bible also served as the philosophical and metaphysical context from which all events, including political events, were interpreted in nineteenth century America (David W. Hall, *Election Day Sermons*, Oak Ridge: Kuyper Institute, 1996, pp. 20–21). The liberty so hard fought for and won was not the libertine humanistic form of licentiousness. It was a true biblical liberty—the freedom to do good as defined by God, not by the arbitrary laws of men. This biblical view of liberty under God and His precepts was the biblical framework declared in the pulpits of America (Ellis Sandoz, *Political Sermons of the American Founding Era 1730–1805*, Indianapolis: Liberty Press, 1991, pp. xiii–xiv).

Election sermons were proclaimed thoughout the legislatures of New England. Thornton said the purpose was to remind the politicians at the beginning of their terms that they needed to rely on Heaven and recognize that Christian morality revealed in the Scriptures was the only sound basis of good law (Thornton, p. xxii).

"Political sermons, triumphalist and doom laden, redolent with biblical imagery and theological terminology, were a feature of the age" (Richard Carwardine, *Evangelicals and Politics in Antebellum America*, New Haven: Yale University Press, 1993, p. ix). We can see that the Revolutionary era clergy's leading political role is not unique. In the mid-nineteenth century, evangelical Christians were the primary agents in shaping American political culture. It was their prior commitment to the Scriptures that informed their political commitments. One minister distilled the question before voters in the 1856 election with great precision. The presidential contest, he declared, was nothing less than a struggle between "truth and falsehood, liberty and tyranny, light and darkness, holiness and sin ... the two great armies of the battlefield of the universe, each contending for victory."

The Founders of America came for freedom—not freedom of trade, but primarily freedom of religion. Religious freedom to obey God and do His will is the fountain from which flow all our other liberties. It is religious liberty that is most precious to the future of our republic and to the proclamation of the Kingdom of God. It is the duty of every generation to preserve and protect these liberties. Thank God for the patriot pastors who stood in their day, pledging their lives, fortunes, and honor to secure our liberty. Though these rights of life, liberty, and the pursuit of happiness are unalienable as far as Heaven is concerned, there are always those minions of Satan who prefer darkness and seek to silence the church. Ministers are the watchmen on the wall who must sound the alarm.

CHAPTER TWO

How Pastors Were Gagged

*His watchmen are blind, they are all
ignorant; they are all dumb dogs, they
cannot bark; sleeping, lying down, loving
to slumber.* —Isaiah 56:10 NKJV

The criticism comes from various quarters. From Christians in the pew to the leaders in Washington there echoes a recurrent question: "Why don't the pastors in the pulpits speak out on the obvious moral and political struggle for the soul of America?"

Marriage is being cheapened by sexual immorality and promiscuity. Our families are under attack, and yet most churches sit on the sidelines. Religious liberties, even the right to publicly proclaim the Gospel, are being assailed, but the church is paralyzed. Our children are being lied to in every class in tax-subsidized public schools and universities—man is merely a cocktail of chemicals that accidentally appeared through time and chance. Our young people despair because all dignity and meaning have been stripped from their existence and they are killing themselves at unprecedented rates, but the church says nothing. Pornography is choking the culture, degrading women, and even exploiting children, polluting the holy act of intimacy reserved for husbands and wives, yet the church does not want to appear "puritanical." While the blood of innocent children streams through the sewers of our cities from babies being violently ripped from their mothers' wombs, the Church stays in its four walls and sings about heaven and having the victory.

In Isaiah's day, the clergy had become corrupt, and their resistance to saying the hard things that begged to be proclaimed was based in greed. *"Yes, they are greedy dogs which never have enough. And they are shepherds who cannot understand; they all look to their own way, every one for his own gain, from his own territory"* (Isaiah 56:11 NKJV). But can we attribute the silence of the Church in our day in America to compromise and backsliding?

Certainly we can find examples of pure cowardice in pulpits. There are church boards who have shackled their preacher with golden handcuffs, and if they speak out on unpopular subjects, they will be fired. There are pastors who also are ignorant of the role of the Church as the stinging prophetic salt. Content only to proclaim half the Gospel ("God loves you"), they refuse to declare that God's love is extended only to those who repent of their sin. Paul taught that Christians, and how much more pastors, are to *"have no fellowship with the unfruitful works of darkness, but rather expose them"* (Ephesians 5:11 NKJV). Paul would often name the names of those who were the enemies of the Truth.

But only a cynic would believe that in the over 300,000 Protestant pulpits in America there are no true pastors who fear God rather than man. Why then are the churches, even the faithful Bible-believing ones, silent?

The enemy of our souls has devised a clever tactic. Christians are, by definition, people under authority. We acknowledge that God is the ultimate authority and that we must submit to Him. We also affirm that God has instituted governments among men and that we must submit to them as well. The IRS code declares that pastors of churches that have the 501(c)(3) tax exemption status cannot speak out in some ways regarding political matters, lest they risk their tax exemption, putting the future of their church at risk. This is a powerful double whammy. First, it has conflicted the conscience of good pastors who do not want to even have the appearance of rebellion. How can they expect their church to respect God's authority and his authority if he, as the pastor, is in rebellion himself? And, because it is not always clear where the boundaries are regarding what you can or cannot say, it has had a chilling effect on all content that might even have the slightest hint of being "political."

It Hasn't Always Been So!

The IRS rule against political activity is a relatively new law. It only dates back to 1954. This restriction is not based in some long-debated, hard-fought struggle to work out a great and noble constitutional principle. In fact, it has nothing to do with the First Amendment or the alleged constitutional requirement to maintain a "wall of separation" between church and state. It is simply one of literally tens of thousands of rules quietly, if not clandestinely, slipped into the tax code. According to James Davidson, who wrote in the Review of Religious Research, it was purely a political move by a power-hungry politician, the then-Senator Lyndon B. Johnson. His motivation was based in his "desire to challenge McCarthyism..., and win re-election." (Larry Witham, "Texas politics blamed for '54 IRS rule; LBJ wanted to keep Senate seat," *Washington Times,* August 27, 1998, p. A4)

Faced with opposition from two powerful anti-Communist nonprofit organizations, Johnson devised a way to silence his opponents four months before the election. He submitted an amendment on the Senate floor to ban all nonprofit groups from engaging in election activity. Without hearings or public debate, his amendment passed the Senate on a voice vote.

Johnson's revision of the federal tax code was targeted at the two organizations contesting his seat, but churches were caught up in the ban. In just minutes and without debate, churches were stripped of their liberty to participate in America's political life.

And while Johnson's ban sparked little opposition in 1954 and is widely accepted today, it departs sharply from the historical role that colonial pulpits played in mobilizing America for war against Britain.

If a church were to use the same language proclaimed in the founding era today, the Internal Revenue Service would come calling. In 1992, the Church at Pierce Creek in Vestal, New York, placed an ad in two newspapers warning Christians not to vote for a particular presidential candidate. Such a vote, the ad warned, in rhetoric echoing antebellum-era preaching, would be tantamount to committing a sin. The IRS took notice, and three years later revoked its tax exemption.

The church argued in court that it was free under the First Amendment to place the ad and that the IRS unfairly targeted it while ignoring partisan activity by churches on the opposite end of the political spectrum. A federal appeals court upheld the IRS revocation, disregarding the church's claim that the IRS engages in selective prosecutions.

A Christian attorney, Mark Troobnick, who represented the church, said there is "no question whatsoever" that the IRS is not evenhanded in its enforcement. He noted that a gubernatorial candidate made a campaign appearance at the Zion African Methodist Episcopal Church in Harlem, New York, in 1994, while the IRS was prosecuting the Church at Pierce Creek. That campaign event made the front page of the *New York Times.* "We submitted to the court dozens and dozens of examples like that," Troobnick said. An erratic and seemingly selective pattern of prosecution continues to this day. Look at this recent report.

Kerry Seeks Support in Black Churches
Talk of Faith, Politics Well Received
John F. Kerry used a Baptist pulpit Sunday to speak of eternal life and denounce President Bush, as Jesse L. Jackson and Al Sharpton joined him for a home-stretch push to energize African American Floridians who felt disenfranchised in 2000. Kerry, who has been reticent about his faith but plans to talk of it more, tried to reach socially conservative blacks put off by his support for civil unions for gay couples by warning against those "who try to divert and push some hot button that has nothing to do with the quality of your life." ... The minister, the Rev. Gaston E. Smith, endorsed Kerry, saying, "To bring our country out of despair, despondency and disgust, God has a John Kerry." (By Mike Allen, *Washington Post,* October 11, 2004.)

Even if you disagree with this particular pastor's opinion, he ought to be able to speak his mind according to the dictates of his conscience. There ought to be no restriction on any pastor, but if this report was accurate, this was a clear violation of the IRS code for 501(c)(3) organizations. This pastor clearly risked his exemption. It ought not to be the case.

The Threat Is Real and Growing
There is a growing trend moving toward more and more restrictions on free speech. It is especially targeted at silencing Christians who have the temerity to obey the Great Commission and call sinners to repentance. In places outside of the U.S. where there is no First Amendment, we

can see what opponents of the Gospel can do to intimidate and censure unpopular speech. Even here in America, where we are supposed to enjoy freedom of speech, we must be vigilant to protect the right to preach the Gospel.

Below is a collection of recent headlines that show the growing encroachment on our freedoms.

Preacher Fined For Anti-Gay Sermon

A PREACHER was found guilty of harassment yesterday, after a gay man complained that his street corner sermon was an incitement to attack homosexuals. (By Simon de Bruxelles, April 25, 2002, www.timesonline.co.uk.)

A Sneak Peek at the Potential of America: An Interview with Pastor Daniel Scot

As a Christian pastor, Daniel Scot escaped the Muslim persecution of Pakistan. Now, under the guise of "hate crimes" legislation, Pastor Scot is now facing persecution for his beliefs in Australia. (By Sam Kastensmidt, August 21, 2003, www.reclaim america.org.)

Verdict in 'Vilifying Islam' Case Exposes Christian Fault Lines

An Australian state tribunal's finding that two pastors had vilified Muslims looks set to widen the divide in the country's Christian community between liberal mainstream church representatives who lauded the ruling and evangelicals who argued that it constituted a dangerous threat to free speech and freedom to evangelize. (By Patrick Goodenough, December 20, 2004, www.cnsnews.com.)

Congress Narrowly Defeats Hate Crime Legislation

Hate Crimes Initiative Defeated in Conference Committee

While working with the Senate to negotiate differences in the 2005 Defense Authorization Bill, House members of the conference committee have defeated the Senate's hate crimes initiative. Senator Gordon Smith (R-OR) originally proposed the amendment to the defense bill, which sought to offer special protections and rights to homosexual victims of crime. Quietly, the measure passed in the Senate before moving to conference. (By Anthony Urti, October 8, 2004, www.reclaimamerica.org.)

Bardot Fined for 'Race Hate' Book

French film legend Brigitte Bardot has been fined 5,000 euros (£3,301) for inciting racial hatred in a book.

The charges against Bardot, 69, related to her bestseller, *A Cry in the Silence,* in which she said she "opposed the Islamisation of France." (www.bbc.com.)

IRS Should Investigate Electioneering by Colorado Springs Catholic Diocese

Bishop Michael Sheridan's Pastoral Letter Designed to Endorse Bush and Other Republican Candidates, Watchdog Group Asserts

Americans United for Separation of Church and State today called on the Internal Revenue Service to investigate electioneering by the Roman Catholic Diocese of Colorado Springs, saying a recent pronouncement by Bishop Michael J. Sheridan may have crossed the line into unlawful partisan politicking. (Americans United for Separation of Church and State, May 27, 2004, www.AU.org.)

Church's Tax-Exempt Status Threatened
Pro-homosexual group lodges complaint with the state against a Montana church that aired the "Battle for Marriage" satellite broadcast.

A Montana church, one of hundreds across the country to broadcast a pro-marriage TV special on May 23, has been threatened by a gay-activists group with removal of its tax-exempt status. (By Steve Jordahl, June 1, 2004, www.alliancedefense-fund.org.)

Leading Catholic Bishop in Spain Speaks Out Despite Threat of Losing Public Funding
"The proposal of a homosexual marriage"... "a grave disorder in the mentality of the prevailing culture."

TOLEDO, Spain—The primate of Spain, Toledo Archbishop Antonio Cañizares Llovera, has said that threats of loss of public funding will not hamper speaking out in truth. While informing Catholic politicians of their obligation to oppose legislation to legalize same-sex unions, the archbishop said of the possible loss of funding: "The Church is able to live in poverty," but not able to live "without proclaiming Jesus Christ and the sole Lordship of God." (July 6, 2004, www.lifesitenews.com.)

Swedish Pastor Sentenced for 'Hate Speech'
CWNews—A lot of people think of Sweden as a 'tolerant' nation. But lately it's starting to show intolerance towards Christianity. A pastor there has been

sentenced to jail for preaching against homosexuality and other sexual sins. (By Dale Hurd, September 10, 2004, www.cwnews.org.)

Two Men Preparing to Carry Crosses Charged with Disorderly Conduct

DAYTON, Tenn.—Before they could get one of their trademark 10-foot wooden crosses fastened together, two men were arrested by Dayton police officers on charges of disorderly conduct at yesterday's Gay Day gathering. The men often travel the nation and the world preaching and carrying the crosses to bring attention to Christianity. They say they are happy for the publicity about their cause. (By Kelli Samantha Hewett, Sunday, May 09, 2005, www.cgi.tennessean.com.)

Christians Face Hearing in Felonies at Gay Rights Event

Four Christian activists face arraignment tomorrow in Philadelphia on felony charges in what they describe as their "peaceful protest" of a homosexual rights event last fall.

The defendants, all members of an evangelical Christian group called Repent America, "exercised their First Amendment rights by preaching the Gospel, and they did it peacefully," said Brian Fahling, an attorney for the American Family Association, who is representing them. (By Joyce Howard Price, January 11, 2005, www.washington-times.com.)

Bible Verses Regarded as Hate Literature

Court rules Scripture exposed homosexuals to ridicule

Certain passages of the Bible can be construed as hate literature if placed in a particular context, according to a Canadian provincial court.

The Court of Queen's Bench in Saskatchewan upheld a 2001 ruling by the province's human rights tribunal that fined a man for submitting a newspaper ad that included citations of four Bible verses that address homosexuality. (By Art Moore, February 18, 2003, www.worldnetnaily.com.)

You would have to be willfully ignorant to see the pattern above and then dismiss it as unimportant to the freedoms we all are called to preserve for ourselves and our children.

Should the Church Remain Silent?

History has rightly been very unkind toward the clergy in Germany under Hitler. The majority of pastors were either co-opted or silenced by the Nazi government. Only a few had the moral clarity to oppose Hitler. Rev. Dietrick Bonhoffer and a few of his fellow pastors were driven underground during WWII because they refused to cooperate with Hitler's murderous regime. Bonhoffer himself was murdered near the end of the war, when it was found out that he was part of a plot to assassinate Hitler. Yet today we consider Bonhoffer a hero and the other pastors cowards.

"What would we have wanted of the church in Germany with the rise of Adolf Hitler?" asked Lynn Buzzard, director of the Church-State Resource Center at Campbell University. "When churches perform their ... traditional task" of addressing moral issues in a political context, "suddenly we say, 'Oh, you've crossed some line.'"

No such line existed at America's founding. If it had, and the clergy had been silent and unwilling to act and lead in the Founding Era, our nation and our liberties might not now exist. Beyond free speech and politically motivated IRS prosecutions is a more fundamental question: Does the Church obey God or man? Should churches submit and obey the law of man and remain silent where the Word of God is not? Thankfully, there is another option.

CHAPTER THREE

The Bill That Seeks to Restore Free Speech in Church

Current IRS statues require that 501(c)(3) organizations, including churches, must "abstain from participating or intervening, directly or indirectly, in any political campaign on behalf of or in opposition to any candidate for public office." A church can be engaged in "issue discussions," but these must be done in a manner so there is no mention any political candidates who hold certain positions on that issue. It is virtually impossible to engage in any meaningful discussion of an issue without bringing in the people who are its advocates or detractors. Of course, politicians would love to keep critics, especially preachers who speak to more people face to face every week than most politicians, from denouncing them for their position on a particular moral matter.

By the way, all laws or "issues" consist of someone's idea of what is good or right. You cannot divorce politics, ethics, and personalities. All laws reflect someone's notion of what is moral. Some object that you cannot legislate morality. That is true in a sense. No law can make a person inwardly righteous. But, in another sense, all law is an assertion of what someone thinks is moral. Corrupt politicians think that the only "moral" thing to do is to do whatever it takes to get re-elected. That is the highest good in their own mind. Others politicians are more principled and try, like our Founders, to follow the laws of nature and of nature's God.

How do we undo the decades of government-sponsored intimidation and selective prosecution of pastors? Below is the text of the bill introduced by Congressman Walter Jones. It might help if you are a lawyer or a bureaucrat to better understand it, but go ahead and read it for yourself. This is arguably the most important piece of legislation we can support in the 109th Congress. This is a significant gateway bill. It will allow pastors to be the burning ministers of righteousness that they were called to be. Once passed into law, the Church would be unshackled from the unjust chains of government intrusion.

HR 235

January 4, 2005

Mr. JONES of North Carolina introduced the following bill, which was referred to the Committee on Ways and Means.

A BILL

To amend the Internal Revenue Code of 1986 to protect the religious free exercise and free speech rights of churches and other houses of worship.

Be it enacted by the Senate and House of Representatives

of the United States of America in Congress assembled,

SECTION 1. SHORT TITLE.

This Act may be cited as the "Houses of Worship Free Speech Restoration Act of 2005."

SEC. 2. HOUSES OF WORSHIP PERMITTED TO ENGAGE IN RELIGIOUS FREE EXERCISE AND FREE SPEECH ACTIVITIES, ETC.

(a) In General—Section 501 of the Internal Revenue Code of 1986 is amended by redesignating subsection (q) as subsection (r) and by inserting after subsection (p) the following new subsection:

'(q) An organization described in section 170(b)(1)(a)(1) or section 508(c)(1)(A) shall not fail to be treated as organized and operated exclusively for a religious purpose, nor shall it be deemed to have participated in, or intervened in any political campaign on behalf of (or in opposition to) any candidate for public office, for purposes of subsection (c)(3) or section 170(c)(2), 2055, 2106, 2522, or 4955 because of the content, preparation, or presentation of any homily, sermon, teaching, dialectic, or other presentation made during religious services or gatherings.'

(b) Effective Date—The amendment made by subsection (a) shall apply to taxable years ending after the date of enactment of this Act.

SEC. 3. CAMPAIGN FINANCE LAWS UNAFFECTED.

No member or leader of an organization described in section 501(q) of the Internal Revenue Code of 1986 (as added by section 2) shall be prohibited from expressing personal views on political matters or elections for public office during regular religious services, so long as these views are not disseminated beyond the members and guests assembled together at the service. For purposes of the preceding sentence, dissemination beyond the members and guests assembled together at a service includes a mailing that results in more than an incremental cost to the organization and any electioneering communication under section 304(f) of the Federal Election Campaign Act of 1971 (2 U.S.C. 434(f)). Nothing in the amendment made by section 2 shall be construed to permit any disbursements for electioneering communications or political expenditures prohibited by the Federal Election Campaign Act of 1971.

Baptist minister Mark Coppenger points out three fundamentally flawed ideas that this bill addresses. "First, it [the government] presumes to say what makes for a proper sermon." Isn't it interesting that even with the right to the freedom of speech and religion guaranteed in the Constitution, politicians think they have the right and spiritual wisdom to know what constitutes proper speech in a church! How the state thinks it knows this better than the church is a puzzle," Coppenger wonders.

"Second," Coppenger continues, "the IRS is reinforcing the woeful impression that Church is only a devotional center and not also a base for cultural reformation." This is a governmental attempt to reduce the claims of Christ to the private sphere of the individual soul. Politicians will allow Christ's kingdom to extend to matters of the family relationships and perhaps even the gathered people of God, but this does violence to the absolute and universal Lordship of Christ over the whole world.

"Third, it ignores a great tradition of naming names," argues Coppenger. If pastors are to be faithful to the glorious biblical heritage of prophetic preaching, then people who do evil, promote evil, or simply allow it must be singled out and confronted. This is every preacher's job!

John the Baptist confronted wicked King Herod for his adulterous cohabitation with his sister-in-law! It cost John his head on a platter, but that was when a notorious, archetypal tyrant ruled. The only rights John "enjoyed" were those granted by the arbitrary dictates of a self-seeking politician. Of course that would never happen today (note: my tongue is firmly ensconced in my cheek). But even if unpopular speech could cost someone his life, it is the duty of the Church to speak out, regardless of the consequences. This is the heritage of the faithful.

When it comes to singling out individual politicians, our Lord Himself indulged in sanctified political name calling. *"On that very day some Pharisees came, saying to Him, 'Get out and depart from here, for Herod wants to kill You.' And He said to them, 'Go, tell that fox, "Behold, I cast out demons and perform cures today and tomorrow, and the third day I shall be perfected."'"* (Luke 13:31–32 NKJV). "Fox" in this context is a pejorative term directed at Herod's fox-like nefarious scheming. If Jesus preached like this today in some churches, He would be rebuked and sent packing!

The Bible is replete with confrontational diatribes against people in power. These messages were the inspired speeches of servants of God directed inside and outside of Israel. From a recalcitrant Egyptian Pharaoh to the proud Babylonian King Nebuchadnezzar, no one was too powerful to avoid the scorching prophetic fire of God's anointed servants. The prophet Samuel announced God's rejection of Israel's very first King Saul. Prophetic messages brought revelation and correction to the very end of Israel's monarchy.

As with John the Baptist, prophets are often scorned, rejected, and without honor. But it is their duty to preach truth without fear of consequences. This is seen in the most holy and perfect example of God's greatest Prophet, Jesus Christ. Falsely charged and maliciously maligned, Jesus, the sinless Son of God, was killed for allegedly speaking blasphemous things. God's prophets, His anointed prosecuting attorneys, sued kings, judges, and priests without regard to their station in life. Even the surrounding Gentile nations were confronted for violating God's moral law and failing their duty to love justice and promote righteousness.

In the ordination of ministers, when they take their vows of allegiance to faithfully serve Christ, it is common for the Isaiah's charge to be read: *"Cry aloud, spare not; lift up your voice like a trumpet; tell My people their transgression, and the house of Jacob their sins"* (Isaiah 58:1 NKJV). Yet the pastors in America are being subverted from their God-ordained duties by the overreaching hand of the federal government.

Coppenger concludes, "Oh, the government will let churches circle the political arena, addressing issues rather than personalities, distributing voting records and such. What it cannot stand is a Nathan marching right up to the adulterous king and accusing, 'You are the man!' What the church, in turn, should not stand is the government conceit that it can penalize such speech while proclaiming itself defender of the biblical sermon." HR 235 will do nothing more than allow religious leaders to educate their flock on the moral issues of the day, whether or not the government considers it political. (Pastor Mark Coppenger, *FIRST-PERSON: HR 235: Ending an Absurdity*, July 29, 2003, Baptist Press.)

James Madison, the architect of the Constitution, in Federalist Ten wrote that he feared that factions might seek to restrict free speech from those who held opposite opinions. The right of free speech would be the antidote for the "mortal diseases" that had destroyed other countries. Aware that elections were often "carried along" by the "vicious arts" of "unworthy candidates," Madison knew that as long as people were free to speak out against unfit candidates, only those with "the most attractive merit and the most diffusive and established characters" would be left. This is precisely the issue at hand in our day! (Douglas Baker, *FIRST-PERSON: HR 235: Freeing the Pulpit,* Tuesday, July 29, 2003, Baptist Press.)

There is an old adage—personnel is policy. Whom a person hires is a statement of what a person values. So too in public life. Whom a community elects as its representative is an extension of its communal values. It is essential that candidates be examined thoroughly and their positions and character be fully vetted. Though this makes for very lively and sometimes negative campaigning, in the end it is the best safeguard against evil persons and policies. Because it is the duty of the pastor to guard God's flock as well as love his neighbors, even unbelieving ones, then he must speak to the matters that impact the community, including issues that impact those who are disenfranchised (the unborn, the poor, the weak, widows, and orphans). But he must also speak to the moral rectitude of particular candidates and their position of the issues.

Who is in office in a particular community is matter for which the Church will be held accountable. *"You are the salt of the earth; but if the salt loses its flavor, how shall it be seasoned? It is then good for nothing but to be thrown out and trampled underfoot by men"* (Matthew 5:13 NKJV). In this life, the unsalty church is marginalized and trampled by men. In eternity, unsalty church members have to account for their failure to be the salt God called them to be. Although we are a nation of laws and not men, it is elected officials that enforce, neglect, and even subvert these laws. A hostile attitude on the part of a few people in power can stop churches in their mission, for example, by restricting building expansion. Elected officials who hire law enforcement can influence the police to look the other way at certain crimes (obscenity, prostitution, etc.). This destroys the quality of life for everyone. Because the Church is not the stinging salt and moral force it ought to be, it is trampled on by those who neither love God nor respect her people.

Character in an elected representative is paramount. The same biblical qualifications that make a person fit to serve in the church ought to apply to the elders who sit in the seat of authority in a city or state. *"An overseer is entrusted with God's work, he must be blameless—not overbearing, not quick-tempered, not given to drunkenness, not violent, not pursuing dishonest gain. Rather he must be hospitable, one who loves what is good, who is self-controlled, upright, holy and disciplined"* (Titus 1:7–8 NIV). This is God's inspired description of a person suitable to lead. The minister of God's Word must be the herald of these standards and be willing and free to call elected officials to measure up.

When the Church speaks and acts like the Church, even when it is in the minority, God can give her great favor and disproportionate influence. In the book of Acts, when Christians were outnumbered one hundred to one, they were respected, if not feared. *"Yet none of the rest dared join them, but the people esteemed them highly"* (Acts 5:13 NKJV). More important than the Church being respected, when the Church is faithful to Christ the name and fame of our Lord will be revered. *"This became known both to all Jews and Greeks dwelling in Ephesus; and fear fell on them all, and the name of the Lord Jesus was magnified"* (Acts 19:17 NKJV).

How do your neighbors perceive the church in your community? Are churches known and respected as the champions of God's Word, proclaiming God's dominion and extending God's grace? Do they serve the community by extending mercy and by seeking elected offices in which to serve the community and bring glory to the Father in Jesus' name? *"Let your light so shine before men, that they may see your good works and glorify your Father in heaven"* (Matthew 5:16 NKJV).

A small but fiercely committed group of Christians in a community can transform it! A community leader once commented about the small church I pastored that they thought we were going to "take over everything." We did make history by helping to elect the first African-American woman to office in our area and had a number of elected officials in our church. In comparison to the mega churches in the community, we were tiny, but, with God's help, we made a very big footprint. With your pastor's moral leadership and example, with the boldness of the Holy Spirit and an attitude of servanthood, your church can reclaim your community for Christ!

CHAPTER FOUR

Congressional Testimony: The Legal Framework for Change

On May 14, 2002, the United States Congress Way and Means Committee held formal hearings on House Resolution 235, the Houses of Worship Political Speech Protection Act. The following are testimonies from taken these hearings, and give the legal, historical and political framework for changing our current laws.

The Testimony of Colby May

Mr. Chairman and members of the Subcommittee on Oversight, thank you for extending the invitation to appear before the Subcommittee to testify in support of H.R. 2357, the "Houses of Worship Political Speech Protection Act," a measure designed to advance free speech and to curb the unbridled discretion of the IRS.

I respectfully request that the entirety of my prepared statement be made a part of the record of today's hearing. The following is an overview of my testimony:

I. Overview

First, replacing the absolute ban on political intervention with the "no substantial part of the activities" test currently used in the lobbying context would not create a loophole in the nation's campaign finance system.

Some critics contend that H.R. 2357 would open a loophole in the nation's campaign finance system. Such criticism, however, is unfounded, since all corporations, including tax-exempt nonprofit corporations, are barred from making "hard money" contributions or any direct or indirect disbursements for "electioneering communications" under the new *Bipartisan Campaign Finance Reform Act of 2002*, which amends the *Federal Election Campaign Act*, 2 U.S.C. §431, *et seq.* The phrase "electioneering communications" boils down to a communication by "means of any broadcast, cable, or satellite communication, newspaper, magazine, outdoor advertising facility, mass mailing, or telephone bank to the general public, or any other form of general public political advertising." *BCFRA* §§ 101(a); 102(b); *FECA* §§ 431(22); 441b(b)(2). These restrictions apply right now and will continue to apply, regardless of any changes to the tax code that may be made by the passage of the "Houses of Worship Political Speech Protection Act."

Second, because there is no clarity on what is a violation of the political intervention ban, having an absolute, one-strike-your-out ban is inherently unjust and unworkable.

The IRS has taken the position that "coded language" violates the political prohibition. *TAM 9117001.* In the publication "Election Year Issues," it explains that "the concern is that [an exempt] organization may support or oppose a particular candidate without specifically naming the candidate by using code words to substitute for the candidates name in its message, such as "'conservative,' 'liberal,' 'pro-life,' 'pro-choice,' 'anti-choice,' 'Republican,' or 'Democrat,' etc. ..." *Exempt Organizations Continuing Education Technical Instruction Program for FY 2002* at 345 ("2002 CETIP"). In a footnote following the text, the IRS notes that it is the "intent" of the party making the communication that will determine whether these "coded words" are to be treated as violations of the political campaign intervention ban:

> A finding of political campaign intervention from the use of coded words is consistent with the word "candidate"—the words are not tantamount to advocating support for or opposition to an entire political party, such as "Republican," or a vague and unidentifiable group of candidates, such as "conservative" because the sender of the message does not <u>intend</u> the recipient to interpret them that way. Coded words, in this context, are used with the <u>intent</u> of conjuring favorable or unfavorable images—they have pejorative or commendatory connotations. [So,] the voter in Vermont, hearing an exhortation regarding "liberal" candidates, may not know who fits that label in Kansas, but presumably he knows who stands for what in Vermont, which is why the coded word is used in the first place. *id.* at 345, n. 10 (underlining added).

As if just dealing with the uncertainty of losing one's tax exemption because "code words" were used wasn't bad enough, the problem is compounded because the IRS here says "intent" is determinative. That position, however, directly contradicts previous statements by the IRS that "intent" or "purpose" is irrelevant in determining whether the political campaign ban has been violated. In its 1993 version of "Election Year Issues," the IRS stated "the motivation of an organization is irrelevant when determining whether the political campaign prohibition has been violated." 1993 CETIP at 414–15. Then, as if this inconsistency over "intent" were not enough confusion on the matter, in its 2002 version the IRS stated:

> Therefore, the resolution of the "bad motive" issue depends upon the way the activity is conducted (the facts and circumstances) [—intent doesn't matter—] and upon any [sic] inquiry into the state of mind of the organization [—intent matters].

2002 CETIP at 351. The only thing that is clear is that the IRS wants the unrestricted discretion to decide it either way. Because a single violation of the political intervention ban requires revocation of exemption, due process and fairness require replacement of the absolute ban with the "no substantial part" standard.[1]

Third, since the beginning of the tax code, churches and houses of worship have been exempt from income taxes because they provide services and promote the general welfare, saving the government the costs of having to do so. That fundamental relationship will not be changed by abandoning the absolute political intervention ban and replacing it with the "no substantial part" test.

Following passage of the Sixteenth Amendment, allowing the federal government to directly tax personal income, churches and houses of worship have been exempt from income taxes. *Tariff Act of 1913*. Congress has always recognized that they are tax exempt, because "the government is compensated for the loss of revenue by its relief from financial burden, which would otherwise have to be met by appropriations from public funds and by the benefits resulting from the promotion of the general welfare." The occasional or incidental, intentional or unintentional, participation by a church, synagogue, or mosque in activities that may be regarded as political campaign involvement will not change this relationship. Passage of H.R. 2357 will not require houses of worship to affirmatively do anything, or fundamentally change their functions. Houses of worship will continue to serve the basic needs of their congregations and their local communities, preserving the historic balance between church and state, and fulfilling the purpose for tax-exemption.

Fourth, given the vague and contradictory positions of the IRS that the same activity can be both permissible for an exempt organization and still violate the political intervention ban, modification of the absolute ban is necessary. The "Houses of Worship Political Speech Protection Act" will both alleviate and obviate the confusion and fear surrounding the requirements for compliance with the political intervention ban. In "Election Year Issues," the tome relied upon by most practitioners in this area as an indicator of the IRS's approach to political campaign activities by exempt organizations, the IRS has taken the view that educational or religious activities which otherwise qualify as exempt activities can nevertheless constitute prohibited political activity:

> The most common question that arises in determining whether an IRC 501(c)(3) organization has violated the political campaign intervention prohibition is whether the activities constitute political intervention or whether they are educational [or religious], purposes for which an IRC 501(c)(3) organization may be formed. ... Sometimes, however, the answer is that the activity is both—it is educational [or religious], but it also constitutes intervention in a political campaign.

2002 CETIP at 349. In a 1989 ruling, the Service stated that "educating the public is not inherently inconsistent with the activity of impermissibly intervening in a political campaign." *TAM 8936002.* Then in a 1999 *Tax Advice Memorandum, 199907021,* the IRS went on to say "even if the organization's advocacy is educational, the organization must still meet all other requirements for exemption. ..." In short, the IRS says you can do it, but you can't. The "Houses of Worship Political Speech Protection Act" will alleviate the deep chill caused by such IRS doublespeak, since whatever the IRS standard is, a one-time step over the line would not result in revocation.

Fifth, modifying the political intervention ban applicable to houses of worship to conform with the "no substantial part" test currently applicable for lobbying activities passes constitutional muster.

In analyzing the constitutionality of a congressional enactment in the Establishment Clause area, the courts continue to use the three-part test articulated in *Lemon v. Kurtzman,* 403 U.S. 602 (1971). See *Lamb's Chapel v. Center Moriches Sch. Dist.,* 508 U.S. 384 (1993) (noting that despite heavy criticism of the Lemon test, Lemon has not been overruled). *See also Jager v. Douglas County Sch. Dist., 862 F.2d 824, 828-29* (11th Cir.), *cert. denied,* 490 U.S. 1090 (1989) (discussing appropriateness of using Lemon test).

Under the Lemon test, "first, the statute must have a secular legislative purpose; second, its principal or primary effect must be one that neither advances nor inhibits religion...; finally, the statute must not foster 'an excessive government entanglement with religion.'" *Lemon,* 403 U.S. at 612-13 (citations omitted). Allowing Congress to determine the application and reach of the tax code fulfills the "secular purpose" element of the *Lemon* test, since only Congress has power under Article I of the Constitution to make and levy taxes. As upheld in *Regan v. Taxation With*

Representation, 461 U.S. 540, 544 (1983), Congress may constitutionally permit certain speakers to be treated differently than others in the context of the tax statute. In *Regan,* the lobbying limits for exempt organizations were upheld against a constitutional challenge, even though different tax-exempt organizations were not subject to the same limitations. As stated in *Rosenberger v. Rector and Visitors of Univ. Of Va.,* 515 U.S. 819, 825 (1995):

> *Regan* relied on a distinction based on preferential treatment of certain speakers—veterans organizations—and not a distinction based on the content or messages of those groups.

Accordingly, allowing Congress to determine the application of the tax code does not violate the secular purpose of the legislation.

Under the second prong of the Lemon test, legislation will violate the Establishment Clause only if its primary effect is to advance or inhibit religion. The effects prong of the Lemon test "asks whether, irrespective of [the] government's actual purpose, the practice under review, in fact, conveys a message of endorsement or disapproval" of religion. *Wallace v. Jaffree,* 472 U.S. 38, 56 n.42 (quoting *Lynch v. Donnelly,* 465 U.S. at 690 (O'Connor, J., concurring)). Modifying the absolute ban on political intervention to conform to the "insubstantiality" test now used in the lobbying test conveys no such endorsement.

Moreover, H.R. 2357 avoids the excessive entanglement of the government with religious institutions, in conformance with the third *Lemon* requirement: "The First Amendment does not prohibit practices which, by any realistic measure, create none of the dangers it is designed to prevent and which do not so directly or substantially involve the state in religious exercises or in the favoring of religion as to have meaningful and practical impact." *Lee v. Weisman*, 505 U.S. 577, 598 (quoting *Schempp*, 374 U.S. at 308 (Goldberg, J., concurring)). In addition, the U.S. Supreme Court has previously upheld the tax exemption for all religious organizations, as *required* in order to avoid the excessive entanglement of the government into the affairs of the church. *Walz v. Tax Commission*, 397 U.S. 664, 671 (1970).[2] It is for all these reasons that "The Houses of Worship Political Speech Protection Act" is constitutional, and a legally appropriate act for Members of Congress to support.

II. Current Law

The phrase "no substantial part of the activities" is found in the current version of the *Internal Revenue Code*, section 501(c)(3), and it relates to the limit of how much "lobbying" or legislative activity a church or exempt organization may conduct. The *Houses of Worship Political Speech Protection Act* (H.R. 2357) uses that same phrase to loosen the absolute ban now applying to any "political activity" (speech or association) by a house of worship.[3]

As a rough rule-of-thumb, the phrase "no substantial part of the activities" has generally come to mean no more than five percent (5%) of an organization's overall expenditures of time, money, and personnel. The five percent (5%) limit also follows the objective expenditure allowances (but a much lower rate) permitted for tax-exempt organizations, but **not** churches or houses of worship, in *IRC 501(h)*, the so-called safe-harbor for lobbying activities.

The "Houses of Worship Political Speech Protection Act" recognizes that no house of worship should be penalized for an occasional or inadvertent statement or action that may be regarded as "political intervention."

III. The Need for the Houses of Worship Political Speech Protection Act

Congressional hearings over the last few years have served to highlight the abuses of the IRS in the name of tax code enforcement. In addition, the IRS has conducted tax or compliance audits of "the Heritage Foundation, Citizens for a Sound Economy, the Christian Coalition, the National Rifle Association, Freedom Alliance, the Western Journalism Center, the National Center for Public Policy, and National Review." (*The Washington Times,* January 8, 1998 at A.7). These and other conservative organizations have been audited as well, while their counterparts in the liberal establishment have gone unscathed.

This type of selective federal investigation and enforcement highlights the need for regulatory reform and deregulation. The point is that no church or house of worship should be penalized for simply speaking out on the issues, candidates, or public leaders; occasionally or inadvertently engaging in activity that may be regarded as political; or accurately providing the voting records and issue stances of elected officials and candidates. Federal agencies such as the IRS cannot become so highly politicized that they become federal arbiters of political thought and permissible speech. The current federal tax code allows the IRS the unbridled leeway and discretion to conduct such politically motivated audits under the guise of regulatory enforcement, and it is using this unbridled discretion in a partisan and selective fashion.

To reign in the IRS's unbridled discretion and bring balance and fairness back to the system, the time has come to change the "*Johnson Amendment.*" This amendment was highly partisan and political and was specifically designed in 1954 by then Senator Lyndon Johnson to "deny tax-exempt status to not only those people who influence legislation, but also those who intervene in any political campaign on behalf of any candidate for any political office."[4] Senator Johnson was angry that two non-profit Texas groups had supported his primary opponent, so he rammed his amendment through the Congress as a floor amendment, without any benefit of a congressional hearing or debate.[5]

The rule has become so intrusive and so significant a threat to the First Amendment rights of all churches, synagogues, mosques, and houses of worship, that total removal of tax exemption can be imposed if a candidate for office addressing a religious body is favorably introduced or is supported from the pulpit. Under the law as written, a one-hour political strategy meeting held on the premises of a church or charity, without paying a market rental, could trigger the complete destruction of the institution by the IRS. A priest who speaks on the moral issues of abortion or capital punishment during a campaign season runs the risk of triggering an IRS investigation or violating the "coded words" restriction. As written, the rule of 501(c)(3) is akin to a highway in which traffic to 65 mph is permissible, but if a motorist goes even 1 mph over the speed limit, the police can arrest the motorist, who would then be subject to the death penalty—an absurd situation. This is not only manifestly unfair, but is also an intolerable infringement by the IRS of the fundamental rights of free speech and the free exercise of religion. It also intrusively entangles the government in religious matters.

The solution is simple. Under current tax law, tax-exempt organizations may carry on lobbying, if their efforts constitute "no substantial" amount of their activities. IRC 501(c)(3). While the term "substantial" is not defined for those entities not making the safe-harbor election permitted under IRC 501(h), such as churches,[6] for over 40 years courts have generally determined that if no more than five percent (5%) of the time and effort of the organization is devoted to lobbying, the lobbying was not "substantial." See

Seasongood v. Commissioner, 227 F.2d 907, 912 (6th Cir. 1955); *World Family Corp. v. Commissioner*, 81 T.C. 958 (1983) (exempt organization's lobbying activities that were less than ten percent (10%)—but more than five percent (5%)—of its total efforts was "insubstantial"). Indeed, Marcus Owen, the former head of Exempt Organizations for the IRS, has been quoted as saying that "the law in this area needs to be clarified, since anything from five percent to *fifteen percent* of total expenditures has been permitted for legislative activity" (*Washington Times*, December 2, 1997, p. A5). From this line of cases and comments, it appears that as long as an organization expends only five percent (5%) or so of its overall expenditures on legislative activity, such activity will be regarded as "insubstantial" and not result in a loss of exemption. Adopting a similar standard for political activity, and amending IRC 501(c)(3) as proposed in the *House of Worship Political Speech Protection Act*, do precisely that.

IV. Tax Exemption Is Linked to Social Policy, Which Leads to the Inevitable Result of Revocation of Tax Exemption for Religious Institutions and Religious Organizations

Ever increasing inroads have been made into the tax-exempt status of religious organizations and churches. Both the IRS and atheist groups have been seeking the revocation of tax-exempt status for religious institutions for some time. See *e.g.*, *Walz v. Tax Commission*, 397 U.S. 664 (1969). Religious institutional doctrine has historically been at odds with social mores that are in vogue. To condition tax exemption on a religious institution's willingness to conform to fashionable ideals (*e.g.*, ordination of homosexuals, same-sex marriages) unavoidably leads to the demise of tax exemption for houses of worship. To avoid this egregious result, it is necessary to modify the tax code and allow a wider berth for houses of worship to generally engage in political speech.

**The Threat to Free Speech and Free Exercise Is Real
Since the IRS Sanctions for Using "Coded Language"
and Is Contradictory on Whether "Intent" Is Relevant**

The Service has taken the position that "coded language" violates the political prohibition. *2002 CETIP* at 344–45. It explains that "the concern is that [an exempt] organization may support or oppose a particular candidate without specifically naming the candidate by using code words to substitute for the candidate's name in its message, such as 'conservative,' 'liberal,' 'pro-life,' 'pro-choice,' 'anti-choice,' 'Republican,' or 'Democrat,' etc. ..." *2002 CETIP* at 345. Then in a footnote, it contradicts its admonition not to use these very "coded words" and states that:

> A finding of political campaign intervention from the use of coded words is consistent with the word "candidate"—the words are not tantamount to advocating support for or opposition to an entire political party, such as "Republican," or a vague and unidentifiable group of candidates, such as "conservative," because the sender of the message does not <u>intend</u> the recipient to interpret them that way. Coded words, in this context, are used with the <u>intent</u> of conjuring favorable or unfavorable images—they have pejorative or commendatory connotations. [So,] the voter in Vermont, hearing an exhortation regarding "liberal" candidates, may not know who fits that label in Kansas, but presumably he knows who stands for what in Vermont, which is why the coded word is used in the first place.*id.* at 345, n. 10 (underlining added).

The confusion and fear surrounding the requirements for compliance with the political intervention ban in section 501(c)(3) are quite real. One need look no further than the guidance pronouncements of the IRS and others in this area. For example, in "Election Year Issues,"[7] the tome relied upon by most practitioners in this area as an indicator of the Service's approach to political campaign activities by exempt organizations, the Service has taken the view that educational or religious activities that otherwise qualify as exempt activities can nevertheless constitute prohibited political activity:

> The most common question that arises in determining whether an IRC 501(c)(3) organization has violated the political campaign intervention prohibition is whether the activities constitute political intervention or whether they are educational [or religious], purposes for which an IRC 501(c)(3) organization may be formed. ... Sometimes, however, the answer is that the activity is both—it is educational [or religious], but it also constitutes intervention in a political campaign. 2002 CETIP at 349.

In a 1989 ruling, the Service stated that "educating the public is not inherently inconsistent with the activity of impermissibly intervening in a political campaign." *TAM 8936002.* Then, in a 1999 *Tax Advice Memorandum, 199907021,* the IRS went on to say, "Even if the organization's advocacy is educational, the organization must still meet all other requirements for exemption." So, the IRS says you can do it, but you can't.

There is also considerable uncertainty over whether one's "intent" or "purpose" in making the communication matters. In its 1993 version of "Election Year Issues," the IRS stated, "the motivation of an organization is irrelevant when determining whether the political campaign prohibition has been violated." 1993 CETIP at 414–15. However, in its 2002 version, the IRS, discussing the debate its 1993 statement generated, stated:

Therefore, the resolution of the "bad motive" issue depends upon the way the activity is conducted (the facts and circumstances) and upon any [sic] inquiry into the state of mind of the organization. 2002 CETIP at 351.

It's clear that the IRS cares about motive or purpose, but then again, it doesn't.[8]

V. The Original Purpose of IRC 501(c)(3) Was to Prevent Political Activism of Non-Profit Groups in Texas During the 1954 Senatorial Campaign of L.B.J.

Tax exemption under IRC 501(c)(3) requires four basic criteria.[9] The chief prohibition amongst these is that nonprofit organizations, including houses of worship, must "not participate in, or intervene in" political campaigns. IRC 501(c)(3). As noted above, this provision was added to the federal tax law in 1954, without benefit of congressional hearings, in the form of a floor amendment in the Senate, 100 Cong. Rec.9604 (1954). During consideration of the legislation that was to become the Revenue Act of 1954, Senator Lyndon B. Johnson of Texas forced the amendment out of his anger that local two Texas non-profit groups had supported his primary opponent. Hopkins, "The Law of Tax-Exempt Organizations," 327 (6th ed. 1992) (hereinafter "Hopkins").

The tax exemptions contained in IRC 501(c)(3) origi- nated as a part of the Tariff Act of 1894. The provision stated that "nothing herein contained shall apply to ... corpo- rations, companies, or associations organized and conducted solely for charitable, religious, or educational purposes" (*i.e.*, houses of worship). After ratification of the Sixteenth Amendment, Congress enacted the Tariff Act of 1913, exempting from the federal income tax "any corporation or association organized and operated exclusively for religious, charitable, scientific, or educational purposes, no part of the net income of which inure to the benefit of any private shareholder or individual."

In the Revenue Act of 1918, the enumeration of tax-exempt organizations was expanded to include those organized "for the prevention of cruelty to children or animals." The Revenue Act of 1921 expanded the statute to exempt "any community chest, fund, or foundation" and added "literary" groups to the list of exempt entities. The Revenue Act of 1924, 1926, 1928, and 1932 did not provide for any changes in the law of tax-exempt organizations.

The Revenue Act of 1934 carried forward the exemption requirements as stated in the prior revenue measures and added the rule that "no substantial part" of the activities of an exempt organization can involve the carrying on of "propaganda" or "attempting to influence legislation." The Revenue Acts of 1936 and 1938 brought forward these same rules, as did the Internal Revenue Code of 1939. The current IRC 501(c)(3) language follows the *"Johnson Amendment"* and came into being upon enactment of the Internal Revenue Code in 1954. 68A Stat. 163 (ch. 736).

VI. The Subsequent Interpretations of IRC 501(C)(3) by the IRS and Courts Makes It Clear That This Portion of the Tax Code Is Meant to Repress Participation in the Political Process

The requirement that a church or charitable organization not engage in political campaign activities has been expanded to prohibit even remotely partisan involvement. In *Christian Echoes National Ministry Inc. v U.S.*, 470 F2d 849 (10th Cir 197. cert. den. 414 U.S. 864 (1973), a federal appeals court denied tax-exempt status to a religious organization for backing a conservative political agenda. The organization, by means of publications and broadcasts, expressed its opposition to candidates and incumbents considered too liberal and endorsed conservative officeholders. The Tenth Circuit summarized the unforgivable offense: "These attempts to elect or defeat certain political leaders reflected ... [the organization's] objective to change the composition of the federal government." *Christian Echoes*, 470 F2d at 856. *See also Monsky v. Comm.*, 36 T.C.M. 1046 (1977); *Giordano v Comm.*,36 T.C.M. 430 (1977). This flat ban on religious involvement in politics is not limited to active campaigning, however. In 1978, the IRS issued a ruling that confined "voter education" activities to those that are nonpartisan in nature. Rev. Rul. 78-248, 1978- 1 C.B. 154.[10]

In a later ruling, the IRS specified the following factors as demonstrating the absence of prohibited campaign activity by a church or nonprofit organization:

1. The voting records of all incumbents will be presented;
2. Candidates for reelection will not be identified;
3. No comment will be made on an individual's overall qualifications for public office;
4. No statements expressly or impliedly endorsing or rejecting any incumbent as a candidate for public office will be made;
5. No comparison of incumbents with other candidates will be made;
6. The organization will point out the inherent limitations of judging the qualifications of an incumbent on the basis of certain selected votes, by stating the need to consider such unrecorded matters as performance on subcommittees and constituent service;
7. The organization will not widely distribute its compilation of incumbents' voting records;
8. The publication will be distributed to the organization's normal readership only; and

9. No attempt will be made to target the publication toward particular areas in which elections are occurring nor to time the date of publication to coincide with an election campaign.

Rev. Rul. 80-282, 1980-2 C.B. 178. The IRS's application of IRC 501(c)(3) then, is to limit any preferential expression for a political candidate. There is no compelling governmental reason to so limit the First Amendment activities of churches and houses of worship. This restriction should thus be modified to track the "insubstantial" standard regarding lobbying and apply that standard to political activity as well.

VII. The IRS Application of the Limitation on Churches Participating in the Political Process Is Expanding, Intrusive, and Selective

Under the First Amendment, the government lacks the license to make determinations about whether a "creed" or "form of worship" is sufficiently "recognized," and whether the church has an adequate organizational structure (*i.e.*, properly ordained ministers, a literature "of its own," etc.) to prevent IRS intrusion and inspection. If "it is not within the judicial ken to question the centrality of particular beliefs or practices of faith" and the "courts must not presume to determine the place of a particular belief in a religion or the plausibility of a religious claim," *Employment Division v. Smith*, 494 U.S. 872, 878 (1990) (citations omitted), it stands to reason that the other branches of the federal government are constitutionally unfit to make those judgments as well. Many independent small churches do not meet regularly, do not have an independent existence, do not have ordained ministers, do not have a formal doctrinal code, and yet nonetheless are churches warranting tax exemption.[11]

Similarly, Treasury regulations describe a church as an

organization with duties that include the "ministration of sacerdotal functions and the conduct of religious worship." Reg. I.51 I-2(a)(3)(ii). This definition begs the question, because it requires Treasury officials to exercise their own judgment in determining what is a priestly function and what is sufficient "religious worship" to qualify for "church" status.

Governmental judgments of this kind are not only unworkable—they are dangerous and unconstitutional. The Supreme Court has reiterated the oft-repeated principle that "religious freedom encompasses the power of religious bodies to decide for themselves, free from state interference, *matters of church government as well as those of faith and doctrine. Serbian Orthodox Diocese v. Milivojevich*, 426 U.S. 696, 722 (1976) (emphasis added); *Kedroff v St. Nicholas Cathedral*, 344 U.S. 94, 116 (1952). In *Corp. of Presiding Bishops v. Amos*, 483 U.S. 327, 341 (1987), Justice Brennan noted: "religious organizations have an interest in autonomy in ordering their internal affairs, so that they may be free to: '*Select their own leaders, define their own doctrines, and run their own institutions*'" (citations and internal quotation marks omitted; emphasis added). Given the weight of constitutional precedent in this area, it defies rationality for the government to empower its tax collecting arm with the ability to invade the religious autonomy of churches while other branches of the government are constitutionally forbidden from doing so.

This is of even greater concern because conservative or orthodox and liberal or reform church organizations are treated quite differently by the IRS. For example, a conservative evangelical church in upstate New York, the Church at Pierce Creek, had its tax exemption revoked in 1995 for impermissible "political" activity. The offending activity involved its published moral and religious stand in the newspaper calling abortions on demand, homosexuality, and premarital sex "sins." "Christians" were admonished to oppose such "sins" and not vote for then-Governor Clinton.[12] Historically, currently, and at the time the Church at Pierce Creek was having its tax-exempt status revoked, numerous churches engaged in similar or more egregious violations, as follows:

Historical Context

1. Since the campaign of Thomas Jefferson, religious and political controversy has been prominent in approximately one of every three campaigns for the presidency. B. Dulce & E. Richter, *Religion and the Presidency* v, 1–11 (1962). *See also* H. Foote, *The Religion of Thomas Jefferson* 45 (1960) (electioneering pamphlets written and distributed by clergymen accused Jefferson of atheism and thus "too dangerous an enemy of Christianity to be president").

2. "During the 1980 election year, a number of religious groups participated in energetic presidential and congressional campaign activities to promote the election of politicians who share their beliefs." Note: "Religion and Political Campaigns: a Proposal to Revise Section 501(c)(3) of the Internal Revenue Code," 49 *Fordham L. Rev.* at 537 (1981) (footnotes omitted).

Political Activity by Churches Where No Sanctions Have Been Levied, But for Which Other Churches Have Had Their Tax Exemptions Revoked

1. "The Reverend Jesse Jackson ... campaigned from pulpits of black churches across the nation in his pursuit of the Democratic nomination" for President in 1984. Reichley, *Religion in American Public Life* 1 (The Brookings Institution, Wash., D.C., 1985).

See also Rosenthal, "Prelates and Politics: Current Views on the Prohibition Against Campaign Activity," Tax Notes 1122 (1991); Chisolm, "Politics and Charity: A Proposal for Peaceful Coexistence," 58 Geo. Wash. L. Rev. (No. 2) 308 (1990); Tesdahl, "Intervention in Political Campaigns by Religious Organizations After the Pickle Hearings—A Proposal for the 1990s," 4 Exempt Org. Tax Rev. (No. 9) 1165 (1991).

2. The IRS Chief Counsel's office "reluctantly" concluded in 1989 that an organization "probably" did not intervene in a political campaign on behalf of or in opposition to a candidate for public office, even though the organization ran a political advertising program that (1) was, in the words of the IRS, "mostly broadcast during a two-week period around the Reagan/Mondale foreign and defense policy debate on October 21, 1984," (2) contained statements that "could be viewed as demonstrating a preference for one of the political candidates" [Mondale], (3) "could be viewed" as having content such that "individuals listening to the ads would generally understand them to support or oppose a candidate in an election campaign," (4) involved statements that were released so close to the November vote as to be "troublesome." IRS Technical Advice Memorandum 8936002. Even though these campaign broadcasts were in clear violation of the IRS's voter education rules, *see e.g.,* Rev. Rul. 86-95, 1986-1 C.B. 332, the IRS nonetheless took no action against this charitable organization for this campaign activity.

3. 9/25/94[13]—Then-Governor of New York Mario Cuomo, President Clinton, and New York Mayor Rudolf Gulliani all campaigned on behalf of

Governor Cuomo from the pulpit of the Bethel A.M.E. Church in Harlem, New York.

4. 10/23/94—Senator Charles Robb and Governor Wilder campaigned on behalf of Senator Robb from the pulpit of the Trinity Baptist Church in Richmond, Virginia.

5. 10/11/94—California Democratic gubernatorial candidate Kathleen Brown campaigned in five different Los Angeles churches: Bethel A.M.E. Church, the Mount Tabor Missionary Baptist Church, the First A.M.E. Church, and the West Los Angeles Church of God in Christ.

6. 11/21/92—Vice President Al Gore campaigned from the pulpit of three different Savannah, Georgia, churches on behalf of Democratic run-off candidate Wyche Fowler.

7. 4/5/92—Presidential candidate Bill Clinton campaigned from the pulpit of the Bridge Street A.M.E. Church in Harlem, New York.

8. 1/27/92—Democratic presidential candidate Tom Harkin campaigned from the pulpit of the Heritage United Church of Christ, located in Baltimore, Maryland.

9. 8/14/90—District of Columbia Mayor Marion Barry campaigned from the pulpit of the Israel Baptist Church.

10. 4/30/90—New York Democratic congressional candidate Charles Shumer campaigned at St. John's Church in New York, speaking with 30 black ministers.

11. 4/98—Democratic congressional candidate contenders Ohio State Senator Jeffrey D. Johnson and Cuyahoga County Prosecutor Stephanie Tubbs Jones campaigned at the Starlight Baptist Church in Cleveland "for an endorsement interview by a black

ministers group." Johnson spent his Sundays campaigning at black churches.

12. 4/8/98—Florida Republican gubernatorial candidate campaigned at Faith Memorial Baptist Church in Liberty City.

13. 3/31/98—Detroit Democratic gubernatorial candidate Doug Ross "announced a 19-member Executive Board of Clergy United for Ross" that was "expected to include 250 ministers by May."

14. 3/8/98—Chicago Democratic gubernatorial candidate Roland Burris campaigned at Chicago churches.

15. 2/22/98—Chicago Democratic gubernatorial candidate Jim Burns "preached his crime-fighting message to South Side parishioners at a storefront church called the House of Refuge."

16. 2/14/98—Democratic congressional candidate Irma Cohen "is relying on Operation Big Vote, the church-based alliance set up by Florida Democrats in 1994 to bring out the black vote. 'The one thing we have going for us is the church network,' Kennedy said. 'Rightly or wrongly, 90 percent of the people in the church do what the minister says.'"

17. 1/6/98—Former Democrat Congressman Rev. Floyd Flake endorsed the congressional candidacy of New York Democratic Assemblyman Gregory Meeks during services at Flakes' Church, the Allen African Methodist Episcopal Church in Jamaica, Queens.

18. 11/13/97, 10/24/97—New Jersey Democratic gubernatorial candidate Jim McGreevy, during the course of his campaign, campaigned in more than 100 churches and made 104 campaign visits to African-American churches.

19. 11/3/97—Both Virginia Democratic gubernatorial candidate Donald S. Beyer, Jr., and Virginia Republican candidate James S. Gilmore, III, campaigned in churches across the state of Virginia.

20. 11/2/97—Roman Catholic Bishop Frank J. Rodimer endorsed New Jersey Democratic gubernatorial candidate Jim McGreevy in his Sunday service homily at St. John's Cathedral in Paterson.

21. 11/1/97, 10/29/97—Executive Director of the Black Ministers Council of New Jersey, Rev. Reginald Jackson, endorsed Republican Governor Christie Whitman, while 24 African-American ministers representing more than 600 churches statewide endorsed Democratic gubernatorial candidate Jim McGreevey.

22. 10/20/97—Rev. Al Sharpton endorsed the candidacy of New York Democratic mayoral candidate Ruth Messinger during Sunday worship services at the Bethel A.M.E. Church in Harlem and at the New Jerusalem Baptist Church in Queens.

23. 10/4/97—Washington Governor Gary Locke made four campaign visits to a Redmond Buddhist Temple, where he was offered sizable campaign donations.

24. 10/4/97—Muslim Amatullah Yamini campaigned in Christian churches in the Onondaga County, New York, State legislative district Democratic primary.

25. 10/2/97—Houston, Texas, Democratic mayoral candidate Lee P. Brown campaigned at the Green Grove Missionary Church.

26. 10/1/97—New York Democratic mayoral candidate Ruth Messinger campaigned at "the Christian Life Center, a 7,000-member nondenominational ministry in Brownsville, Brooklyn."

27. 5/15/97—The Black Clergy of Philadelphia, repre-

senting 450 churches, announced their choices for judicial candidates at the Vine Memorial Baptist Church. The clergy members were joined by many of the candidates they were endorsing.

28. 12/9/96—At the Houston, Texas, Windsor Village United Methodist Church: "The message to God came just after U.S. Rep. Richard Gephardt of Missouri, the Democratic leader of the U.S. House, asked the audience to support the reelection of Democratic U.S. Rep. Ken Bentsen." Rep. Gephardt and Rep. Bentsen then proceeded to campaign at a Chinese Baptist church and several African American churches in Houston.

29. 11/11/96—As the *Denver Post* plainly put it: "Don't try to tell a black minister about the separation of church and state. Not when the state comes striding into the sanctuary nearly every Sunday, begging for votes. ... Other political and religious leaders in Denver say far more candidates than Webb owe their elections to northeast Denver and the political work of black churches there. They say Tim Wirth and Gary Hart could not have won their U.S. Senate races without an all-out effort from the church congregations."

30. 11/5/96—U.S. Senator Paul Simon campaigned at the Grace United Methodist Church in Springfield, Illinois, on behalf of Democratic congressional candidate Dick Durbin.

31. 11/5/96—Rev. Jesse Jackson campaigned on behalf of Rhode Island Democratic candidates at the Pond Street Baptist Church in Providence.

32. 11/4/96—President Clinton campaigned at the St. Paul AME Church in Tampa, Florida.

33. 11/4/96—Democratic Rep. Martin Frost "made campaign stops at four African-American churches

[during Sunday services] in southeast Fort Worth, Texas."

34. 11/4/96—Louisiana Democratic Senatorial Candidate Mary Landrieu "visited African-American churches Sunday, including Asia Baptist Church, where she received an enthusiastic endorsement from the Rev. Zebadee Bridges."

35. 11/4/96—North Carolina Democratic "Senate Candidate Harvey Gantt visited five black Charlotte congregations on Sunday, mounting the pulpit in three. ... 'There comes a time in a campaign when you have to trust the voters to do the right thing,' he said from the pulpit, 'I'm not going to beat up on Senator Helms. ... All I'm going to say is, he's been there 24 years. That's enough time.'"

36. 11/4/96—Pastor Joe Fuiten of the Cedar Park Assembly of God Church in Seattle, Washington, urged his congregants to vote for Republican candidates, while across town at the Mount Zion Baptist Church, Rev. Samuel B. McKinney urged his church members to vote the Democratic ticket.

37. 11/4/96—Democratic Senatorial candidate Mark Warner campaigned in African American churches across the state of Virginia.

38. 11/3/96—Democratic Memphis Mayor Herenton endorsed Democratic congressional candidate Harold Ford, Jr., at the Greater Imani Church, in Memphis, Tennessee.

39. 10/28/96—The Northeast Ministers Alliance, an organization of 60 mostly African American churches located in Houston, Texas, endorsed a slate of Democratic candidates running for various state-level offices, and one Republican running for local sheriff.

40. 10/21/96—President Clinton campaigned at the

New Hope Baptist Church in Newark, New Jersey.

41. 9/17/96—"The Greater Denver Ministerial Alliance, representing more than 100 black churches and 20,000 Denver voters, endorsed Bill Clinton for president, Al Gore for vice president, Democrat Ted Strickland for the Senate, and Republican Joe Rogers for the House."

42. 9/13/96—Reverend Acen Phillips endorsed the candidacy of Republican congressional African American candidate Joe Rogers, at the Mount Gilead Baptist Church in Denver, Colorado.

43. 8/26/96—Vice President Al Gore campaigned with the Rev. Jesse Jackson at the Fellowship Baptist Church in Charleston, North Carolina. The Rev. Jackson is co-minister of the church.

44. 11/8/95—U.S. Democratic Rep. Cleo Fields campaigned for governor at a New Orleans church.

45. 9/15/95—Several Orthodox rabbis spoke from the pulpit in favor of Baltimore Democratic mayoral primary candidates.

46. 8/12/95—"The influential and powerful United Ministerial Coalition of Baltimore threw their thousands of affiliated church members behind the re-election effort of [Baltimore] Mayor Kurt L. Shmoke."

47. 5/18/95—Gubernatorial candidate Kentucky Senate President John "Eck" Rose campaigned at the Canaan Missionary Baptist church in Louisville, Kentucky.

48. 2/28/95—Philadelphia Mayor Edward G. Rendell picked up a re-election endorsement from the Black Clergy of Philadelphia & Vicinity, representing more than 400 churches and ministries. The endorsement "was formally announced at a press conference in the basement of the Vine Memorial

Baptist Church in West Philadelphia."
49. 2/6/95—Chicago Democratic primary mayoral candidate Joe Gardner campaigned at the St. Stephen's African Methodist Episcopal Church, on Chicago's West Side.
50. 11/7/94—Rev. Jesse Jackson campaigned on behalf of Democratic candidates at the New Hope Church of God in Christ in Norfolk, Virginia.
51. 11/6/94—Republican Senatorial Candidate Ollie North and Democratic Senatorial incumbent Charles Robb both campaigned at Virginia churches.
52. 11/3/94—President Clinton campaigned for Democratic candidates at the Antioch Baptist Church in Cleveland, Ohio.
53. 10/31/94—New Jersey Democratic Senator Frank Lautenberg campaigned at the Salem Baptist Church in Jersey City.
54. 10/24/94—Former Virginia Gov. Douglas Wilder campaigned for Virginia Senator Charles Robb at the Trinity Baptist Church.
55. 10/13/94—New Jersey Democratic Senator Frank Lautenberg was endorsed by a group of 30 ministers at a news conference held at the Zion AME Church in Brunswick, New Jersey.
56. 7/19/94—Democratic Rep. Maxine Waters campaigned at Detroit's Dexter Avenue Baptist Church on behalf of Michigan Democratic gubernatorial candidate Howard Wolpe.
57. 6/2/94—Democratic Governor Mario Cuomo campaigned at the St. John Baptist Church in Buffalo, New York.
58. 5/13/94—Democratic Governor Mario Cuomo campaigned at "the Hillcreat Jewish Center in Queens, a Conservative shul, to Temple Emmanuel

on Fifth Avenue, a Reform synagogue, and wrapped up his evening at the Orthodox Union dinner at the Grand Hyatt Hotel."

VIII. The IRS Should Not Have Unbridled Discretion

Clearly, churches and houses of worship engage in "political activity." However, the IRS uses its authority selectively to target only those it wishes to silence or threaten. Today it may be orthodox and conservative views, but tomorrow it could be liberal or unconventional views. Such unbridled discretion not only creates constitutional concerns, but it also illustrates why Congress needs to reign in the IRS to ensure constitutional compliance and lift the sword of Damocles hanging over churches. The Supreme Court has "previously identified two major First Amendment risks associated with unbridled licensing schemes: self-censorship by speakers in order to avoid being denied a license to speak [or having one withdrawn]; and the difficulty of effectively detecting, reviewing and correcting content-based censorship as applied without standards by which to measure the licensor's action." *City of Lakewood v. Plain Dealer Publishing Company*, 108 S. Ct. 2138, 2145 (1988).

In *Shuttlesworth v. City of Birmingham*, 394 U.S. 147, 153 (1969), the court also explained: "We have consistently condemned licensing [or regulatory] schemes which vest in administrative officials discretion to grant or withhold a permit upon broad criteria." This is the heart of the problem that has been created due to the IRS's discretion and selective application of the law. It is precisely the absence of sufficient clear and specific standards by which to gage the qualifications and conduct of houses of worship in the political activities area that needs to be corrected. Otherwise, government officials may unconstitutionally "pursue their personal predilections."

IX. A Simple Revision to the Tax Code Will Alleviate This Problem

The IRS's enforcement and regulation of the "political" activities of houses of worship is discriminatory and improperly based upon its "predilections" of the moment: one church is permitted to say something, but another is not; one's activity is appropriate, but the same activity by another is not, etc. To avoid this type of arbitrary or capricious enforcement, and remove the dramatic chilling impact the IRS's selective enforcement has, the *Houses of Worship Political Speech Protection Act* proposes a substantiality test for this type of "political activity," as is currently the case with regard to legislative or lobbying activity by churches and houses of worship.

Present Language of IRC 501(c)(3):

The following organizations are [exempt from taxation under this subtitle]:

Corporations and any community chest, fund, or foundation, organized and operated exclusively for religious charitable, scientific, testing for public safety, literary, or educational purposes, or to foster national or international amateur sports competition (but only if not part of its activities involve the provision of athletic facilities or equipment), or for the prevention of cruelty to children or animals, no part of the net earnings of which inures to the benefit of any private shareholder or individual, no substantial part of the activities of which is carrying on propaganda, or otherwise attempting, to influence legislation (except as otherwise provided in subsection (h)), *and which does not participate in, or intervene in (including the publishing and distribution of statements), any political campaign on behalf of (or in opposition to) any candidate for public office.*

Proposed Change to IRC 501(c)(3) in the *Houses of Worship Political Speech Protection Act*:

The following organizations are [exempt from taxation under this subtitle]:

Corporations, and any community chest, fund, or foundation, organized and operated exclusively for religious charitable, scientific, testing for public safety, literary, or educational purposes, or to foster national or international amateur sports competition (but only if not part of its activities involve the provision of athletic facilities or equipment), or for the prevention of cruelty to children or animals, no part of the net earnings of which inures to the benefit of any private shareholder or individual, no substantial part of the activities of which is carrying on propaganda, or otherwise attempting to influence legislation (except as otherwise provided in subsection (h)), and *except in the case of an organization described in section 508(c)(1)(A) (relating to churches), which does not participate in, or intervene in (including the publishing and distribution of statements), any political campaign on behalf of (or in opposition to) any candidate for public office and, in the case of an organization described in section 508(c)(1)(A), no substantial part of the activities of which is participating in, or intervening in (including the publishing or distributing of statements), any political campaign on behalf of (or in opposition to) any candidate for public office.*

X. Conclusion

Given the historic and critically necessary role churches and houses of worship have played in speaking to the issues of the day, and with the continuing desire of many religious people in the United States to speak out collectively on matters of moral importance, the time has come to rectify a nearly 50-year-old injustice and to change IRC 501(c)(3), as proposed in the *Houses of Worship Political Speech Protection Act.*

[1] The courts have repeatedly held that when a regulatory agency has conflicting interpretations or applications of its rules and regulations, due process is violated because no clear or fair notice of what is required for compliance has been given. *Satellite Broadcasting Co., Inc. v. FCC*, 262 U.S. App. D.C. 274, 824 F.2d 1 (D.C. Cir. 1987); *General Elec. Co. v. EPA*, 311 U.S. App. D.C. 360, 53 F.3d 1324, 1327 (D.C. Cir. 1995); *United States v. Chrysler Corp.*, 332 U.S. App. D.C. 444, 158 F.3d 1350, 1354-57 (D.C. Cir. 1998) (holding that the agency failed to provide fair notice of specific requirements of compliance and therefore could not move to enforce its regulations); *Rollins Envtl. Svcs. (NJ) Inc. v. EPA*, 290 U.S. App. D.C. 331, 937 F.2d 649, 653 (D.C. Cir. 1991) (rescinding a fine assessed by the EPA because the regulation was ambiguous); *Gates & Fox Co., Inc. v. OSHRC*, 252 U.S. App. D.C. 332, 790 F.2d 154, 156 (D.C. Cir. 1986) (holding that agency failure to give fair notice of its interpretation of its regulations precluded enforcement); *Trinity Broadcasting of Florida, Inc., et al. v. FCC*, 211 F3d 618, 2000 U.S. App. LEXIS 8918 (D.C. Cir. 2000) (same).

[2] The concern over entanglement is also why churches and houses of worship, pursuant to IRC 6033(a)(2), need not file annual informational tax returns (IRS Form 990), while all other exempt organizations must.

[3] Section 501(c)(3) of the Internal Revenue Code has been interpreted by courts to prevent even a *single* activity that might be regarded as "participating in, or intervening in" a political campaign on behalf of or in opposition to a candidate for public office. *Association of the Bar of the City of New York v.* Commissioner, 858 F.2d 876 (2nd Cir, 1988); *Branch Ministries v. Rossotti*, 40 F. Supp. 2d 15 (D.D.C. 1999); *aff'd*, 211 F.3d 1137 (D.C. Cir. 2000).

[4] 100 Cong. Rec. 9604 (1954).

[5] *See* Hopkins, *The Law of Tax-Exempt Organizations* at 327 (6th ed. 1992) (herein "Hopkins").

[6] Churches are not permitted to make the election for lobbying activities pursuant to IRC 501(h)(5). This exclusion means that the lobbying activities of churches are governed by the "substantial part test," which is a facts and circumstances evaluation. IRS Reg. 1(a)(4); *Kentucky Bar Foundation, Inc. v. Comm'r*, 78 T.C. 971 (1982) (the issue of "substantial[ity]" is a question of facts and circumstances). Moreover, for the same reason that churches need not file an annual tax return (IRC

6033(a)(2))—to avoid government entanglement—so too churches may not make the IRC 501(h) election.

[7] Judith Kindell and John F. Reilly, "Election Year Issues," Exempt Organizations Continuing Education Technical Instruction Program, www.irs.gov ("2002 CETIP Text").

[8] The courts have repeatedly held that when a regulatory agency has conflicting interpretations or applications of its rules and regulations, due process is violated because no clear or fair notice of what is required for compliance has been given. *Satellite Broadcasting Co., Inc. v. FCC*, 262 U.S. App. D.C. 274, 824 F.2d 1 (D.C. Cir. 1987); *General Elec. Co. v. EPA*, 311 U.S. App. D.C. 360, 53 F.3d 1324, 1327 (D.C. Cir. 1995); *United States v. Chrysler Corp.*, 332 U.S. App. D.C. 444, 158 F.3d 1350, 1354–57 (D.C. Cir. 1998) (holding that the agency failed to provide fair notice of specific requirements of compliance and therefore could not move to enforce its regulations); *Rollins Envtl. Svcs. (NJ) Inc. v. EPA*, 290 U.S. App. D.C. 331, 937 F.2d 649, 653 (D.C. Cir. 1991) (rescinding a fine assessed by the EPA because the regulation was ambiguous); *Gates & Fox Co., Inc. v. OSHRC*, 252 U.S. App. D.C. 332, 790 F.2d 154, 156 (D.C. Cir. 1986) (holding that agency failure to give fair notice of its interpretation of its regulations precluded enforcement); *Trinity Broadcasting of Florida, Inc., et al. v. FCC*, 211 F3d 618, 2000 U.S. App. LEXIS 8918 (D.C. Cir. 2000) (same).

[9] That is, organizations described in IRC 170(c)(2)(B), 501(c)(3), 2055(a)(2), 2106(a)(2)(A)(ii) and (iii), and 2522(a)(2) and (b)(2).

[10] This ruling was a reversal of a prior ruling wherein the IRS stated that the prohibitions against involvement in political campaigns "do not refer only to participation or intervention with a partisan motive, but to *any* participation or intervention which affects voter acceptance or rejection of a candidate." Consequently, the IRS determined that "the organization's solicitation and publication of candidates' views on topics of concerns to the organization can reasonably be expected to influence voters to accept or reject candidates." Rev Rul.78–I 60. 1978–1 C.B. at 154 (emphasis added). This flat ban on all First Amendment activity relating to politics engendered a public outcry and a rare reversal by the IRS. Hopkins at 332.

[11] Indeed, by the standards that the IRS applies today, Jesus and the Apostles would not qualify for "church" status. *See* Internal Revenue Service Manual 321.3 (outlining the 14-point test used by the IRS to determine "church" status).

[12] *Branch Ministries v. Rossotti*, 40 F. Supp. 2d 15 (D.D.C. 1999); *aff'd*, 211 F.3d 1137 (D.C. Cir. 2000).

[13] The cited dates are the dates of articles about the church campaign events, not necessarily the dates of the events themselves.

The Testimony of
Dr. D. James Kennedy

Good afternoon, Mr. Chairman. Thank you for the opportunity to be here. On behalf of the thousands of people who have signed petitions asking Congress to pass the Houses of Worship Political Speech Protections Act—some of which you see stacked on the table before me—I am pleased to have this opportunity to address the subcommittee.

In the summer of 1954, Lyndon B. Johnson had a problem: What to do about powerful anti-Communist organizations threatening his Senate reelection. The answer proved amazingly simple. Just like Congress this past spring, Johnson figured out that the best way to deal with these "special interests" was to silence them.

So, on July 2, 1954, as the Senate considered a major tax code revision, Johnson offered a floor amendment to ban all nonprofit 501(C)(3) groups from engaging in political activity. Without hearings or public debate, his amendment passed the Senate on a voice vote. Johnson's revision to the federal tax code was targeted at the nonprofit groups contesting his seat, but churches were caught up in the ban. In just minutes and without debate, churches, for reasons that had nothing to do with the separation of church and state, were stripped of their liberty to participate in America's political life.

That will change if "The Houses of Worship Political Speech Protection Act," introduced by Rep. Walter Jones and cosponsored by 114 other Members, becomes law. Jones' bill will reverse Johnson's ban and return the protection of the First Amendment to America's churches, synagogues, and mosques. Today, the hearing that never took place 48 years ago is convening as the House Ways and

Means Oversight Subcommittee considers this bill.

This legislation is a vitally important step in reversing a long-standing injustice whereby free speech seems to be protected everywhere except in the pulpits of our churches and other houses of worship. It will restore to churches a freedom and role that dates to America's infancy. Nineteenth century historian John Wingate Thornton said that "in a very great degree, to the pulpit, the PURITAN Pulpit, we owe the moral force which won our independence."

The British would agree. Disgusted at the black-robed clergy's prominent role in stirring the colonies to fight, the Redcoats called them the "Black Regiment." And Prime Minister Horace Walpole declared in Parliament that "Cousin America has run off with a Presbyterian parson." Walpole was most likely referring to John Witherspoon, who was a Presbyterian minister, president of Princeton and a signer of the Declaration of Independence. Witherspoon, who was accused of turning his college into a "seminary of sedition," was the most important "political parson" of the Revolutionary period, according to the Library of Congress.

During the Revolutionary era, graduates of Yale and Harvard, serving in churches across New England, laid out the theology of resistance that made war with Britain inevitable. One of the most provocative and influential sermons preached was Jonathan Mayhew's 1750 "Discourse Concerning Unlimited Submission and Non-Resistance to the Higher Powers." His message, quickly printed and read on both sides of the Atlantic, justified political and military resistance to tyrants and has been called "The Morning Gun of the American Revolution."

When British General Thomas Gage attempted to silence the incendiary messages being preached by New England's Black Regiment, one clergyman, William Gordon, declared in defiance that "There are special times and seasons when [the minister] may treat of politics." To do otherwise was not possible for New England's ministers, who had been faithfully applying God's Word to every area of life since the first generation arrived in Massachusetts.

In the mid-nineteenth century, evangelical Christians were primary agents in shaping American political culture, according to Richard Carwardine, author of *Evangelicals and Politics in Antebellum America.* "Political sermons, triumphalist and doom laden, redolent with biblical imagery and theological terminology, were a feature of the age," he writes.

For example, one minister distilled the question before voters in the 1856 election as a contest pitting "truth and falsehood, liberty and tyranny, light and darkness, holiness and sin … the two great armies of the battlefield of the universe, each contending for victory."

Language like that today might earn a visit from the Internal Revenue Service. It did in 1992, after the Church at Pierce Creek in Vestal, New York, placed a newspaper ad warning Christians not to vote for Bill Clinton for president. Such a vote, the ad warned, in rhetoric echoing 1856, would be to commit a sin. The IRS took notice, and three years later it revoked the church's tax exemption.

Aggressive toward Pierce Creek, the IRS has, at other times, looked the other way. In 1994, for example, New York Governor Mario Cuomo campaigned for reelection on a Sunday morning at the Bethel African Methodist Episcopal Church in Harlem. "Cuomo was rewarded with a long, loud round of applause and an unequivocal endorsement from the pastor," according to a *Newsday* report. The American Center for Law and Justice, which represented the Church at Pierce Creek, uncovered evidence at trial that the IRS knew of more than 500 instances where candidates appeared before churches, as happened with Gov. Cuomo and Bethel A.M.E., but took no action to revoke these churches' tax-exempt status.

The unequal enforcement of the existing law is just one of several reasons why scrapping the political activity ban altogether is a good idea. The political activity restriction is a blatant violation of the First Amendment, is vague and burdensome, and marginalizes churches at a time when America most needs a moral compass.

The First Amendment states that "Congress shall make no law respecting an establishment of religion, or prohibiting the free exercise thereof; or abridging the freedom of speech." Yet that is exactly what the Congress has done by silencing churches.

Nor is the political activity ban easy to obey. Not just endorsements, but voter education activities, such as voter guides that compare office-seekers on issues, may violate the ban if they are perceived as partisan. Even addressing moral concerns, such as abortion, from the pulpit during an election campaign may violate the IRS rule if abortion, for example, is under debate in the campaign.

With so much uncertainty and so much at risk, silence is, regrettably, the only option for the minister who wants to ensure that the IRS does not open a file on his church. But when Caesar's demand for silence confronts the message of God's Word, ministers are forced into hard choices. That's what happened in Nazi Germany a generation ago. Many pastors submitted and were silent. Others were not and paid the price.

If, as has been asserted, we owe our liberties to the "moral force" of the pulpit, the censorship of that voice— for reasons that have everything to do with partisan politics and nothing to do with the separation of church and state— is a monumental mistake that should be quickly corrected. In a culture like ours, which sometimes seems on moral life support, the voice of the Church and her message of reconciliation, virtue, and hope must not be silenced.

The Testimony of William E. Fauntroy

Chairman Houghton and members of committee, my name Walter E. Fauntroy. I am in my forty-third (43rd) year as pastor of the New Bethel Baptist Church here in our nation's capital. Over the course of those years, I have had the privilege of being at the core of nearly every major change in public policy in this country affecting people of African descent.

In the decade of the 1960s I served as Director of the Washington Bureau of Dr. Martin Luther King, Jr.'s Southern Christian Leadership Conference. In that capacity I coordinated our activities for both the Historic March on Washington in 1963 and the Selma-To-Montgomery Voting Rights March of 1965. I was Dr. King's chief lobbyist for passage of the Civil Rights Act of 1964 and the Voting Rights Act of 1965.

In the decades of the 1970s and '80s I served as a member of this august body as the District of Columbia's first Delegate to the U.S. House of Representatives in 100 years. During my twenty year tenure as a member of the House Banking, Finance, and Urban Affairs Committee, I had the great privilege of being chairman of the subcommittee on Domestic Monetary Policy and then the subcommittee on International Development, Finance, Trade and Monetary Policy.

What I have learned as a pastor, civil rights activist and member of congress over these years has led me to appear before you today in support of H.R. 2357, the Houses of Worship Political Speech Protection Act. In the five minutes allowed me, I want to share with you two definitions of "politics" upon which I have acted over these years as a pastor, as a civil rights activist and as a politician that inform my decision to support this legislation.

The first definition is this: *"Politics is the means by which we in a democracy translate what we believe into public policy and practice;"* that is, we go to the polls to vote for people who, when elected, promise to translate what we believe into public policy and practice. That right to vote is so precious to me because, as an African American, I am painfully aware how racist white voters in the Southland, by denying my people the right to vote, were able to translate into public policy and practice what they believed. They believed that black people, for example, should not be allowed to drink water from the same public fountains used by white people; and with their votes, they translated that into public policy and practice.

A second definition of politics upon which I have always acted is that *"Politics in the process by which we determine who gets how much of what, when and where in five areas: income, education, healthcare, housing and justice."* In fact, during my twenty year tenure in this Congress, I became thoroughly conversant with our nation's fourteen cabinet level agencies and their counterparts in the standing committees of the U.S. House and Senate, agencies and committees that determine who gets how much and what, when and where in agriculture, in commerce, in labor and housing and health and human services, for example. That's what I have learned as a politician.

Let me tell you what I have learned as a thoroughly trained pastor. I have learned from the Prophet Isaiah that the basic tenet of my Judeo-Christian-Muslim heritage is that we are all *"anointed of God to declare good news to the poor, to bind up the broken hearted and to set at liberty them that are bound" (Isaiah 61:1).* You can understand, therefore, that as a citizen who has a right to vote to translate what he believes into public policy and practice and as a man whose faith dictates that he seek to provide "the least of these" access to adequate income, education, healthcare, housing and justice, I never have and I never will allow any one to deny me that right to vote my beliefs at the polls. I have not and I will not allow any one deny me my right to try to persuade as many fellow citizens as I can reach to vote as I do.

There is, therefore, no election—local, state or national—where I think that the plight of the "least of these" is at stake that I do not endorse a candidate of my choice in an effort to influence the members of my congregation and any one else who I think values my opinion on matters of public policy. That is my right both as a citizen and a man of faith, and I will defend that right even for those people of faith with whom I vehemently disagree as to how income, education, healthcare, housing and justice should be distributed in our society.

Now I must also tell you that it is not in my interest nor is it in the interest of the people whom I serve that certain people who call themselves "religious" benefit from the passage of HR 2357. That's because it has been my experience that people often use religion and race as excuses for denying to others the income, education, healthcare, housing and justice that they covet for themselves. In our Judeo-Christian-Muslim heritage we call that "sin" which, defined, is the arrogance and self-seeking of man.

Mr. Chairman and members of the committee, take it from someone who knows, people who call themselves religious, when it comes to their greed and opportunism, will often talk East and walk West on you in the arena of public policy. They say one thing and they do another. Jesus called such people *"false prophets who come to you in sheep's clothing, but inwardly they are ravening wolves" (Matt. 7:15).* Ku Klux Klansmen are false prophets who use Christianity as an excuse to deny black people access to income, education, healthcare, housing and justice. Muslim extremists like Osama Bin Laden are false prophets who use Islam as an excuse to kill other people to deny them access to income, education, health care housing and justice. In so doing, they distort Islam and blaspheme the name of Allah. Zionists extremist are false prophets who use Judaism as an excuse to take from others what they covet for themselves: income, education, healthcare, housing, and justice.

They all come up with cute excuses for their ungodly actions but they are not correct. They appear to be sincere but they are sincerely wrong. The right thing for all Jews, all Christians and all Muslims to do is recorded in their own holy writ in the words of Micah 6:8 – *"He hath shown thee O man, what is good; and what doth the Lord require of thee, but to do justly, and to love mercy, and to walk humbly with thy God?"*

So, Mr. Chairman, I know that it is not in my interest or that of the people whom I serve that certain people who are self-centered hypocrites when it comes to the basic tenets of their religions exercise their right to be wrong. But like Voltaire, I may disagree with them vehemently, but I will defend to the death their right to be wrong and their right to participate in an orderly effort to "translate what they believe into public policy and practice." I must not be selfish and, therefore, sinful; I must not demand for myself what I would deny others. I believe that he who would *"save his life, shall lose it; and he that loses his life for my sake shall find it."***(Matthew 10:39)**

I support the passage of H.R. 2357. Thank you.

The Testimony of William Wood

It is fascinating that there are hearings on the 501(c)3 status of churches and their ability to engage in political speech. On the one hand, every perversion, foul word, and form of pornography passes as "free speech" under the pretense that no one dare tread on this liberty. Yet "free speech" is not so free in the province and domain of religious institutions. The First Amendment did not suggest that there was "free speech" except for churches and pastors. Yet somehow we have interpreted "freedom of religion" to have both speech prohibitions and religious prohibitions through IRS regulations. This paper approaches the entire subject of IRS regulation from the standpoint of why is political speech restricted at all in a church? How has "freedom OF religion" been converted to "freedom FROM religion" in the political sphere by the use of IRS code?

A more preliminary investigation as to whether or not a 501(c)3 designation and IRS regulation is in order.

> *Separation of church and state today goes beyond the simple non-coercion approach of the founders. What appears to be happening is that government (e.g., the defendant in the Good News Club case) appears to be affirmatively hostile to religion. Many people rightly sense three things: (1) the exclusion of religion from the public square threatens liberty by stunting the formation of moral consciences; (2) the exclusion of religion also threatens liberty by requiring government to use government power to enforce secular norms of morality; and (3) the exclusion of religion in the name of neutrality is false and discriminatory when the government then chooses to endorse and*

promote a secular morality that is offensive to the very people excluded from the debate. As applied, the notion of the wall of separation between church and state, rather than removing government from the morality game, just picks certain winners and losers, a result that the founders sought to avoid.[1]

The door of the Free Exercise Clause stands tightly closed against any governmental regulation of religious beliefs as such.[2] Government may neither compel affirmation of a repugnant belief;[3] nor penalize or discriminate against individuals or groups because they hold religious views abhorrent to the authorities;[4] **nor employ the taxing power to inhibit the dissemination of particular religious views**.[5]

Our "American" legal system and government have, in fact, done exactly that which has been prohibited. We have enacted special IRS rules, regulations, and procedures, under the guise of a "501" *et. al.* status, for churches. Our Founding Fathers, many of them men of faith, would have seen this as a direct assault on the First Amendment. With "free speech" in America, anything goes, but with Freedom of Religion, ONLY that endorsed, approved, and stamped with the IRS 501 approval qualifies.

Yet there is no "compelling state interest" for regulating the political speech of churches through backdoor means, through a 501, or any other IRS status:

The Supreme Court has applied "strict scrutiny" to government actions burdening free exercise of religion, requiring the government to show that its action serves a compelling state interest and is the least restrictive means for achieving the government objective...[6] *If there is any fixed star in our constitu-*

*tional constellation, it is that no official, high or petty, **can prescribe what shall be orthodox in politics, nationalism, religion, or other matters of opinion** or force citizens to confess by word or act their faith therein.*[7]

Yet this continued encroachment on "political speech" and restriction on "endorsing political candidates" are precisely what the IRS designations aim to assert. As if to imply that in a DEMOCRACY, the people hearing a message from the pulpit are too stupid, too frail, or too intimidated to exercise an opinion contrary to the utterances from the pulpit. These restrictions are simple anti-Christian exercises of restriction on free speech by banning certain types of speech by religious institutions. Of course, they are under threat of losing their tax-exempt status. I am constantly amazed by the "ACLU's" (I question how "American" they really are) incessant attacks on anything even remotely resembling Christianity, yet proclaiming that perversions such as NAMBLA (the North American Man Boy Love Association, who believes in homosexual sex with little boys eight years old) as "Free Speech." Apparently there are few, if any, restraints on free speech AS LONG AS IT DOES NOT OCCUR IN A CHURCH!

What if a pastor, with sincere conviction and belief, were to speak a particularly pointed message against a particular politician, or a particular bill in the context of: "For we wrestle not against flesh and blood, but against principalities, *against powers, against the rulers of the darkness of this world, **against spiritual wickedness in high places***"?[8]

What of those times when a pastor, near election time, considers the particular actions of a legislator, where that legislator has endorsed a particularly reprehensible proposition? Say, for example, the partial birth abortion debate where a baby's head is exposed from the womb, stabbed in the head with a sharp object, and then its brains are sucked out until the head collapses. What if a minister of faith considers this a particularly reprehensible evil that must be spoken against from the pulpit, naming specifically those individuals, considering them "rulers of darkness" or practicing "spiritual wickedness in high places"? What of a bill introduced would allow for homosexual marriages, or the right to consortium with animals, or with children such as that NAMBLA espouses, or other reprehensible legislation. Must they IGNORE their conscience, and their religious beliefs, and the tenets of their faith to satisfy an IRS that would now DICTATE this is impermissible speech? Why is the IRS, an arm of the Federal government, entangled in the regulation of religion to dictate and determine what is acceptable political speech? Is this not a "breach" in the fictitious "wall of separation"?

Or the reverse, where a particular politician or legislator is openly praised through "supplications, [public] prayers... and giving of thanks":

> I exhort therefore, that, first of all, supplications, prayers, intercessions, and giving of thanks, be made for all men; for kings, and for all that are in authority; that we may lead a quiet and peaceable life in all godliness and honesty. For this is good and acceptable in the sight of God our Saviour.[9]

So we now have codified provisions, that based on the honest, sincere, rights of conscience, free exercise of religion, and freedom of speech where these ideals may be attacked. And where men and women of conviction or virtue may have their speech silenced BECAUSE of their religious affiliation that allows them the "tax-exempt" status.

How can we have "free speech" and "freedom of religion" with a few IRS bindings and shackles on religious speech? WHY do we use the IRS to regulate supposedly "free" speech in the "free exercise of religion"?[10]

What "Separation of Church and State"?

We have erected anti-Christian barriers to religion in America under the fraudulently constructed guise of "Separation of Church and State." This often-quoted phrase is used as an excuse to ATTACK every display of anything founded upon the Judeo-Christian biblical beliefs. Yet it is a LEGAL FRAUD!

Thomas Jefferson WAS NOT IN THE COUNTRY FOR THE CONSTITUTIONAL DEBATES OVER THE FIRST AMENDMENT MAKING EXCERPTS FROM A LETTER OF HIS VOID. "Of [the Constitutional] convention Mr. Jefferson was not a member, he being then absent as minister to France."[11] In fact, as noted in the U.S. Supreme Court case just quoted from, Jefferson "expressed his disappointment at the absence of an express declaration insuring the freedom of religion." Somehow Jefferson's idea of "freedom OF religion" has been twisted and perverted into a legal fiction almost demanding "freedom FROM religion" in politics. Our legal system has inappropriately given weight to the anti-Christian "separation of church and state" phrase. In according so much "authority" to this phrase, equal weight must be given to the remaining letters, lest the legal system finally seen as declaring open war on Judeo-Christian beliefs, most especially one in which Jefferson strictly forbid the use of his own letters as a source of constitutional interpretation:

> *On every question of construction [of the Constitution] let us carry ourselves back to the time when the Constitution was adopted, recollect the*

spirit manifested in the debates, and instead of trying what meaning may be squeezed out of the text, or intended against it, conform to the probable one in which it was passed.[12]

Even more distressing and exposing the passionate anti-Christian perspective of the modern "American" legal system, and the proponents of the often taken out of context "separation of church and state" are the sheer number of state legislatures whose Constitutions openly endorsed Judeo-Christian principles AFTER THE FIRST AMENDMENT WAS PASSED. Mysteriously, they found no conflict in their own constitutional constructions:

Massachusetts; First Part, Article II (1780) "It is the right as well as the duty of all men in society, publicly, and at stated seasons, to worship the SUPREME BEING, the great Creator and Preserver of the universe. ... The governor shall be chosen annually; and no person shall be eligible to this office, unless...he shall declare himself to be of the Christian religion." Chapter VI, Article I (1780) "[All persons elected to State office or to the Legislature must] make and subscribe the following declaration, viz. 'I,_____, do declare, that I believe the Christian religion, and have firm persuasion of its truth...'"

New Hampshire; Part 1, Article 1, Section 5 (1784) "...the legislature ... authorize ... the several towns ... to make adequate provision at their own expense, for the support and maintenance of public Protestant teachers of piety, religion and morality." Part 2, (1784) "[Provides that no person be elected governor, senator, representative or member of the Council] who is not of the Protestant religion."

Pennsylvania; Article IX, Section 4 (1790) "that no person, who Acknowledges the being of a God, and a future state of rewards and punishments, shall, on account of his religious sentiments, be disqualified to hold any office or place of trust or profit under this commonwealth."

Tennessee; Article VIII, Section 1 (1796) "...no minister of the gospel, or priest of any denomination whatever, shall be eligible to a seat in either house of the legislature..."; Section 2 "...no person who denies the Being of God, or a future state of rewards and punishments, shall hold any office in the civil department of this State."

Are we as American people to believe that Massachusetts, New Hampshire, Pennsylvania, and Tennessee endorsed Judeo-Christian principles in their Constitutions but somehow ratified the U.S. Constitution with this implicit "freedom FROM religion" as practiced in the legal system today? Or what of the other colonies who already had Constitutions with similar provisions BEFORE the adoption of the U.S. Constitution and then did not set about to immediately change their Constitutions? The question for every person of faith in this country is why there is such a passionate hatred for Christianity and Judeo-Christian beliefs that this country was founded upon. And why there has been such a concerted effort to encroach upon the domain of the church by REGULATING A CHURCH'S POLITICAL SPEECH.

Even other legal scholars and Federal judges know of the outright legal FRAUD perpetrated on the Christian faith in America. Judge Brevard Hand, a Federal District judge, stated the "Supreme Court erred in its reading of history."[13] In fact, after this rather embarrassing exposé, the U.S. Supreme Court left off relying on the intent of the framers, clearly demonstrating their anti-Christian bent and re-created the original Legal Fraud under a principle called the "crucible of litigation."[14] As applied in this case, the "crucible of litigation" in laymen's terms is translated to mean that, whether we have constructed an anti-Christian fraud or not, we will not back down from our improper interpretation of the historical foundations[15] of this country's Christian heritage. In fact, in analyzing this case, Rhenquist noted:

> *But the greatest injury of the "wall" notion is its mischievous diversion of judges from the actual intentions of the drafters of the Bill of Rights. The "crucible of litigation"... is well adapted to adjudicating factual disputes on the basis of testimony presented in court, but* **no amount of repetition of historical errors in judicial opinions can make the errors true**. *The "wall of separation between church and State" is* **a metaphor based on bad history**, *a metaphor which has proved useless as a guide to judging. It should be frankly and explicitly abandoned.*[16]

America was founded as a Christian nation,[17] "one nation under God," with coins that read, "In God We Trust." Before the U.S. Supreme Court and the U.S. legal system became so antagonistic toward Christianity, it declared, "We are a Christian people[18] according to one another the equal right of religious freedom, and acknowledging with reverence the duty of obedience to the will of God."[19]

The U.S. Supreme Court, in all of its anti-Christian zeal, has recently struck down the Religious Freedom Restoration Act,[20] insisting that Congress had violated the separation of powers doctrine. Yet it has ignored its previous precedents to ensure the legal fraud; Congress "remains free to alter what [this Court has] done;"[21] and the Judiciary has enacted its own legislation to guarantee that it can break the law at will[22] by giving itself "immunity." Yet there is no rush in the Judiciary to abandon its own self-legislated immunity to break the law as it sees fit (all the while somehow declaring the violating the law must be some form of "judicial function").

Until the unprecedented attack on Christian morals, values, and beliefs in the U.S. legal system in the last 40 +/- years, it was well understood that "Christianity and democracy are not separable if democracy is to persist."[23]

And WHY do we use the IRS to regulate supposedly "free" speech in the "free exercise of religion"?[24]

Why Attack the Christian Foundations of America?

Many of those (though, unfortunately, not all) who wage war on the Christian foundations of this country do so out of ignorance or a predisposition to creating and generating more government power and control. Most judges and elected representatives do not consciously conceive of ways to undermine the country's foundations and values. In fact, the greatest problem in all three branches of government is a lack of basic principles and understanding that our Founding Fathers were well aware of.

In evaluating the recent *Wallace v. Jaffree* opinion undermining the Religious Freedom Restoration Act, an interesting legal philosophy emerges—the replacement of unalienable rights with civil rights. The court relied heavily on "Civil Rights" contained in the 14th Amendment. In the last 40+ years there has been an accelerated use of "Civil Rights" as a means to undermine and destroy our Founder's concept of unalienable rights.

This whole concept of unalienable rights comes from the Declaration of Independence where our Founding Fathers sought to throw off the bands of tyranny and oppression: *"We hold these Truths to be self-evident, that all Men are created equal, that they are endowed by their Creator with certain unalienable rights..."*

Inalienable (or unalienable) rights "cannot be transferred or surrendered"[25] and include "natural rights," which *"exist independently of rights created by government or society*, such as the right to life, liberty, and property,"[26] as well as "natural law," which contains *"legal and moral principles... [or] divine justice rather than from legislative or judicial action*; moral law embodied in principles of right and wrong."[27]

And then the 14th Amendment was created, after the 13th Amendment (which abolished slavery) noting:

> *No State shall make or enforce any law which shall abridge the privileges or immunities of any citizen of the United States; nor shall any State deprive any person of life, liberty, or property without due process of law; nor deny to any person within its jurisdiction the equal protection of the laws.*

The 14th Amendment became the basis of Civil Rights, or civil law for the United States. Civil Rights are "the individual rights of personal liberty guaranteed by the Bill of Rights and by the 13th, 14th, 15th, and 19th Amendments, as well as by legislation... Civil rights include especially... the right of due process, and the right of equal protection under the law."[28] Civil Liberty is a part of Civil Rights denoting "freedom from UNDUE governmental interference or restraint [as determined by government, of course]. This term usually refers to freedom of speech or religion."[29] Civil Rights are also part of the Civil Law, which is *"the body of law IMPOSED BY THE STATE, as OPPOSED to moral law."*[30] One of the signers of the Constitution noted the intention of American law stating, "Far from being rivals or enemies, religion and law are twin sisters, friends, and mutual assistants. Indeed, these two sciences run into each other. The divine law, as discovered by reason and the moral sense, forms an essential part of both."[31]

As the 14th Amendment is incorrectly applied today, it is in direct opposition to the "Creator-endowed unalienable rights" guaranteed by our originally enacted Constitution. Where there are "Creator-endowed unalienable rights," there is the requirement to determine the Creator who endowed them so that the rules are clear. This principle was widely understood and clearly known throughout the early history of our country, until it came under direct attack by the lawyers in black robes in our courts today. As Thomas Jefferson noted, "Nothing ... is unchangeable but the inherent and inalienable rights of man."[32] To the extent that they are changeable, such as under Civil Rights interpretations by the lawyer-led courts, they are no longer unalienable rights. The clearest example of this can be seen with the whole abortion debate. A brand new "civil" right was created to allow the killing of babies on demand, even to the point of stabbing a partially born human child in the head and then sucking its brains out. This is a "state"-created, state-endorsed, and state-sponsored right that can be altered at any time. That is why we hear shrieks of horror at the prospect of a Supreme Court Justice who might not be favorable to this state-created right. Under "Creator-endowed unalienable rights," stabbing a partially born human child in the head and sucking its brains out would be a seditious evil demanding of criminal prosecution for those carrying out such heinous acts.

To gain and keep power and control, the black-robed lawyer-led judiciary MUST maintain and promote Civil Rights as opposed to unalienable rights. Civil Rights give the courts their power over issues that our Founding Fathers would be horrified to see today. Civil Rights allow the "back-door control" of churches through state-created "statuses" such as the IRS code in question here. The exercise of unalienable rights takes power and control away from both the state and the courts. So frightening is the prospect of unalienable rights to the lawyer-led judiciary that all vestiges of unalienable rights MUST be drawn under their control and domain. To gain civil control, Bibles MUST be banned from the classroom (the very rule book for the unalienable rights), political speech MUST be stopped from the pulpit (to stifle and stop morality, values, and any virtuous influence in politics), and the 10 Commandments and every biblical reference in our Nation MUST be torn down and removed from EVERY place in the Nation.

As a direct result of the blatant attack on the Foundations of this Nation's religious history, America now enjoys an unprecedented place in history. Of the industrialized nations, we are now:

#1 In Teen Pregnancy
#1 In Violent Crime
#1 In Prison and Jail incarcerations
#1 In illiteracy
#1 In Suicide
#1 In Divorce
#1 In Drug Use

And the list goes on and on. Yet the frightening part of all of this is that it serves a CIVIL government well. The more social disorder, chaos, immorality, violence, crime, and other ills suffered by society, the greater need for more and more government control, and the greater and greater need for the growth of government to "combat" the ills that its attack on America's foundations created to begin with.

"Can the liberties of a nation be thought secure when we

have removed their only firm basis, a conviction in the minds of the people that these liberties are the gift of God?"[33]

The principles of our Founding Fathers were simple: they believed that if one abided by the "Golden Rule" and preserved a sense of community based in common morals, values, and virtues, little government would be needed.

Please take a moment and read some of the quotes from our Founding Fathers and then ask yourself, would THEIR interpretation of the Constitution allow the IRS to regulate a church's political speech?

> *Only a virtuous people are capable of freedom. As nations become corrupt and vicious, they have more need of masters.*[34]
>
> *Neither the wisest constitution nor the wisest laws will secure the liberty and happiness of a people whose manners are universally corrupt.*[35]
>
> *It is religion and morality alone which can establish the principles upon which freedom can securely stand. The only foundation of a free constitution is pure virtue.*[36]
>
> *If we and our posterity reject religious instruction and authority, violate the rules of eternal justice, trifle with the injunctions of morality, and recklessly destroy the political constitution which holds us together, no man can tell how sudden a catastrophe may overwhelm us that shall bury all our glory in profound obscurity.*[37]
>
> *"Religion, morality, and knowledge ... [are] necessary to good government and the happiness of mankind."—Northwest Ordinance (1787)*
>
> *We have no government armed with power capable of contending with human passions unbridled by morality and religion. ... Our constitution was made only for a moral and religious people. It is*

wholly inadequate to the government of any other.[38]
*The law given from Sinai was a civil and munici-
pal as well as a moral and religious code; it
contained many statutes ... of universal application-
laws essential to the existence of men in society, and
most of which have been enacted by every nation
which ever professed any code of laws.*[39]

*No free government now exists in the world,
unless where Christianity is acknowledged, and is
the religion of the country.*[40]

*The doctrines of Jesus are simple, and tend all to
the happiness of mankind.*[41]

And WHY do we use the IRS to regulate
supposedly "free" speech in the "free exercise of
religion"?[42]

---

[1]Wendall Hall. March 28, 2001.

[2]Sherbert v. Verner, 374 U.S. 398, 402 (1963) citing *Cantwell v.
Connecticut,* 310 U.S. 296, 303.

[3]Sherbert at 402 citing *Torcaso v. Watkins,* 367 U.S. 488.

[4]Sherbert at 402 citing *Fowler v. Rhode Island,* 345 U.S. 67.

[5]Sherbert at 402 citing *Murdock v. Pennsylvania,* 319 U.S. 105; *Follett v.
McCormick,* 321 U.S. 573 ; cf. *Grosjean v. American Press Co.,* 297
U.S. 233.

[6]*Employment Div., Dep't of Human Resources v. Smith,* 494 U.S. 872,
881–82 (1990); *Yoder,* 406 U.S. at 233 (1972); *Sherbert v. Verner,* 374
U.S. 398, 402 (1963).

[7]*West Virginia Bd. of Educ. v. Barnette,* 319 U.S. 624, 642 (1943).

[8]Ephesians 6:12.

[9]1 Timothy 2:1–4.

[10]Constitutional rights, such as liberty, are not suitable objects for taxation **or encumbrances**. *West Virginia v Barnette,* 319 U.S. 624; *U.S. v*

Euge, 444 U.S. 707.

[11]*Reynolds v. U.S.,* 98 U.S. 145, 163 (1878).

[12]Thomas Jefferson, letter to Justice William Johnson, June 12, 1823, *The Complete Jefferson,* p. 322.

[13]*Jaffree v. Board of School Comm. of Mobile Co.,* 554 F. Supp. 1104, 1128 (1983).

[14]*Wallace v. Jaffree,* 472 U.S. 38, 52 (1985).

[15]"No understanding of the eighteenth century is possible if we unconsciously omit, or consciously jam out, the religious theme just because our own milieu is secular. ... Religion was a fundamental cause of the American Revolution." —Mitre and Sceptre, Oxford University Press, 1962.

[16]*Wallace v. Jaffree,* 472 U.S. 38, 52 (1985).

[17]Common Law is the traditionally accepted means of interpreting the U.S. Constitution consistent with the intent of the framers. The following are judicial authority for the proposition that Christianity is part of the common law in the United States: *Shover v. State,* 10 Ark. 259 (1850); *State v. Chandler,* 2 Har. 553 (Del. 1837); *State v. Bott,* 31 La. Ann. 663 (1879); *Pearce v. Atwood,* 13 Mass. 324 (1816); *Lindenmuller v. People,* 33 Barb. 548 (N.Y. 1861); *Updegraph v.Comm.,* 11 5. & R. 394 (Pa. 1882); *Charleston v. Benjamin,* 2 Strob. 508 (S.C. 1846); *Bell v. State,* 1 Swan 42 (Tenn. 1851); *Grimes v. Harmon,* 35 Ind. 198 (1871); *Melvin v. Easley,* 52 N. C. 356 (1860); *Judefind v. State,* 78 Md. 510, 28 Atl. 405 (1894).

[18]*U.S. v. MacIntosh,* 283 U.S. 605 (1931) citing *Holy Trinity Church v. United States* 143 U.S. 457, 470, 471 S., 12 S. Ct. 511.

[19]*U.S. v. MacIntosh,* 283 U.S. 605 (1931).

[20]*City of Boerne v. Flores,* 521 U.S. 507 (1997).

[21]*Patterson v. McLean Credit Union,* 491 U. S. 164, 173 (1989).

[22]**"Official immunity doctrine, which "has in large part been of judicial making," *Doe v. McMillan,* 412 U.S. 306, 318-319 citing *Barr*** v. *Matteo,* 360 U.S. at 569. Yet this concept was rejected by Mr. Thomas Jefferson as well when he stated, "It is error [or abuse] alone which needs the support of government. Truth can stand by itself."

[23]*Stephens, School, Church and State* (1928) 12 MARQ. L. REV. 206.

[24]"A (government) may not impose a charge for the enjoyment of a right granted by the federal constitution." *Murdock v Pennsylvania,* 319 U.S. 105; 113.

[25]*Black's Law Dictionary* (2000 abridged edition) p. 1060 and 1061.

[26]*Black's,* p. 1061.

[27]*Black's,* p. 841.

[28]*Black's,* p. 195.

[29]Ibid.

[30]Ibid., definition 3.

[31]James Wilson, *The Works of the Honourable James Wilson* (Philadelphia: Bronson and Chauncey, 1804), Vol. I, p. 106.

[32]Thomas Jefferson to J. Cartwright, 1824.

[33]Thomas Jefferson, *Notes on Virginia,* 1782.

[34]Benjamin Franklin, *The Writings of Benjamin Franklin,* Jared Sparks, editor (Boston: Tappan, Whittemore and Mason, 1840), Vol. X, p. 297, April 17, 1787.

[35]William V. Wells, *The Life and Public Service of Samuel Adams* (Boston: Little, Brown, & Co., 1865), Vol. I, p. 22, quoting from a political essay by Samuel Adams published in *The Public Advertiser,* 1749.

[36]John Adams, *The Works of John Adams, Second President of the United States,* Charles Francis Adams, editor (Boston: Little, Brown, 1854), Vol. IX, p. 401, to Zabdiel Adams on June 21, 1776.

[37]Daniel Webster, *The Writings and Speeches of Daniel Webster* (Boston: Little, Brown, & Company, 1903), Vol. XIII, p. 492. From "The Dignity and Importance of History," February 23, 1852.

[38]*The Works of John Adams, Second President of the United States,* Vol. IX, p. 229, October 11, 1798.

[39]John Quincy Adams, *Letters of John Quincy Adams, to His Son, on the Bible and Its Teachings* (Auburn: James M. Alden, 1850), p. 61.

[40]Pennsylvania Supreme Court, 1824. *Updegraph v. Cmmonwealth;* 11 Serg. & R. 393, 406 (Sup.Ct. Penn. 1824)—such a modern profession by a judge would be ridiculed and criticized, and the judge making such a statement would be attacked and maligned.

[41]Thomas Jefferson, *The Writings of Thomas Jefferson*, Albert Bergh, editor (Washington, D.C.: Thomas Jefferson Memorial Assoc., 1904), Vol. XV, p. 383.

[42]The exercise of religion is not a suitable basis for taxation. *Follett v McCormick,* 321 U.S. 573. The mere chilling of a constitutional right is held oppressive. *Shapiro v Thompson,* 374 U.S. 618.

CHAPTER FIVE

What You Can Do to End the Gag Order

An Army of One

In the section below I will spell out for you what you can do to be a major influence in your community on this and other issues. None of this is new; these are the tried and true ways of moving elected officials on any issue.

If you have access to the Internet, go to www.HR235.org to see if the bill sponsors have been listed. If you can't find the list, personally contact your congressman and find out his position on the bill. Do not assume that you know his or her position based on prior votes or political party. You must not discredit yourself by moving forward on hearsay or defective information. Common courtesy requires that you give your public servants the opportunity to speak for themselves. See the back of the book on how to find the contact information for your elected representatives.

When you call your local congressional office, ask to speak to the congressman directly. Don't be intimidated.

This is a public servant elected to represent you! You have every right—even a duty—to hold him accountable. Always be polite, but don't be afraid even to respectfully disagree. Often a congressman will be home on Fridays in his district when Congress is in session. If he is not coming home to the district soon, call his office in Washington, D.C. You will be asked what you are calling about. Be sure you know the bill number, HR 235. If you get the congressman on the phone, respectfully ask him for his position, for or against.

Oftentimes you will not get the congressman directly, especially if he is opposed to the bill. If his staff says that they do not have an answer, kindly let them know you will be calling back in a week and that you will expect for them to know. Let them know that if they do not have the answer in a week, you will assume that they are opposed to the bill. Get the name of the staffer you spoke to and record the date and time you called and the result of your call. Let that person know that you are documenting the call. This helps to keep everyone accountable.

If you call back in a week and they say they still don't know the congressman's position, then let them know that you are forced to conclude that congressman is opposed to the bill and simply does not want to be on record. If they object, inform them that you know that they have access to the congressman and that they have no excuse. Document the name of the staffer and the date and time and result of your call.

If he supports the bill, take the time to thank him. We are often quick to complain but seldom praise our elected officials. If he supports the bill, he can do more than just vote the right way. Ask him to be listed as a sponsor. Write a letter thanking him. Copy the letter to both offices, local and in D.C. Produce a short letter to the editor (approximately 100 words), and send it to the local newspapers, secular and religious, and let people know of his position. Ask people to contact him and thank him and, if applicable, urge him to become a sponsor. Let your friends know at work, school, church, Sunday school, or home group. Show them what you have done and ask them to do the same.

Remember that just a handful of fiercely committed people can have a great influence. In San Diego, where I am from, there is a group that meets monthly, made up of mostly retired women, called Women's Volunteers in Politics (Women's VIPS). Anna Dewey has organized a great team of phone callers, letter writers, and faxers that have learned how to hold elected officials' feet to the fire!

If your congressman does not respond or outright opposes the bill, politely but firmly express your disappointment. Send him a certified letter or send a fax and keep a copy of the transmission record recounting the process you went through with names, dates, etc. Tell him that you would like to urge him to reconsider his position in favor of the bill and that you intend to make his opposition or support public.

Always keep a copy of any letter or fax you send. Be sure to mail and/or fax it to both his D.C. office and his local office. Just last week in D.C., I bumped into a friendly congresswoman whom we had been trying to reach for weeks. She said she had no idea we were trying to contact her! This was a friendly contact! Imagine if we were confronting her on some important issue that she wanted to duck.

When dealing with congressional staff, assume nothing, document everything, send multiple copies, and save your originals! Don't be shocked, but some staffers withhold information and then lie about it! Those who do not want to be accountable have a way of losing letters. Sometimes staffers are just doing what they are told and are running interference so that they can protect their boss from awkward situations. Don't take it personally; just be smart and don't take "I don't know" for an answer.

Do not always assume that the congressman is evil (this takes great self-control sometimes), but is just ill-informed. So do him a favor and send him a copy of *Gag Order.* Again, be sure to send it by certified mail or drop it off at his office. Get the name and business card of the staff person who receives it. Write down the date and time you dropped off the book. You might even ask for a picture of yourself handing them the book, if you can get them to agree. If they are opposed, they will probably refuse!

Politely let them know that you are going to inform the public of his position. Give them a week to read the book. They will make excuses if they want to hide. Don't let them tell you a week is too soon. If it is important, they will take the time to read it.

If, after this very patient and fair process, they are still opposed or playing games, you must do a couple of simple things. Write a letter to the editor of all your local papers. You would be surprised how sensitive a politician is to being criticized in the newspaper. Sometimes all it takes is this one thing to get them to change their position.

Call in to local talk radio on religious and secular stations. This is a bit unnerving the first time. Be sure you have all your facts in front of you in case you are asked, for instance, the dates and times you contacted the congressional offices and their response! Have the talking points listed on page 108 ready when you call. This will really get the congressman's attention!

If you really want to give your congressman heartburn, organize a rally in front of his local offices. Congressmen absolutely hate this! Send out a written notice or fax to the local papers and radio and TV stations. Make sure they receive it at least by the day before and let them know your intentions to protest the congressman's office. Set a time to speak to the press so that they have it ready for the evening news, no later than 3:00 or so. The press loves a good fight! You really need only a dozen or so people to get the press out, but of course, the more the merrier. Make some bright homemade posters with a few pithy slogans on them. The TV crew will be glad to show them. Using the talking points provided at the end of this chapter, do a press conference. Expose your representative as one who does not support freedom of speech.

Whenever you deal with the press, you must be firm, but not hysterical! The media love to portray people of faith in a negative light, and often we provide them all the ammunition they need. Invite your pastor and other ministers to come and make a comment. If there are other elected officials that support your position, invite them. Politicians need to be seen in the press, and many of them might want to take advantage of the opportunity. By the way, this will really scare the congressman. He might think he will have to run against some other local elected official who is on the right side of this issue. It takes only about ten to twenty minutes to do this well. Have a prepared statement one to two minutes long. Then let the pastors and elected officials speak. Practice answering the common questions listed below. Always try to smile and be pleasant. Keep some extra copies of this book to give to the press when they show up.

Of course, it would be wonderful if you could get your pastor involved. Take a copy of *Gag Order* to your pastor and let him know that his congressman or senator supports keeping ministers from being able to use their First Amendment right of free speech. Hopefully he will see the threat and respond accordingly. Ask your pastor if he can communicate this concern to the other ministers with whom he has a relationship, both within and outside of his denomination or circles. (Offer to buy a quantity of books for him to take to the next ministers meeting.) See if there are any pastors' groups or clergy councils that you can come and

speak to for just five minutes. Perhaps there are other organizations that might have an interest in seeing ministers
regain their rights who will invite you to speak, such as
Sunday school classes. Ask if they will send out an e-mail to
their list and encourage their constituents to call the
congressman.

Most congressmen go to Washington, D.C., and seldom
hear from the very people who voted them into office. A
dozen or so phone calls, faxes, or even e-mails in their home
district will definitely get their attention. You can make that
happen with your circle of influence.

We at the Center for Reclaiming would love to hear
about what you have done! You can come to our Web site at
www.reclaimamerica.org and tell us. We might post it on the
Web, so be sure to take good pictures, too. When the bill gets
closer to being voted on, we will be sending out Center
Alerts with the latest developments and practical things you
can do to make a difference. Go to the Web site and sign up
for Center Alerts! Join our grassroots coalition, and let's
unshackle our pastors. We can do it with the help of committed people like you.

Talking Points

- HR 235 is about recognizing the need to return a
  stolen right from our nation's houses of worship.
  Prior to 1954, churches were free to speak out
  about any and every topic—without government
  limitations.
- Since the "Johnson Amendment," the IRS has had
  a gag order over houses of worship that forbids
  religious leaders to speak out on the moral issues
  of the day. If found in violation of this law, the
  church, mosque, or synagogue would be in jeop-
  ardy of losing its tax-exempt status.

- HR 235 will do nothing more than allow religious leaders to educate their flock on the moral issues of the day, whether considered political or not. This legislation has to do with the issue of speech and nothing else.

- Those in opposition of this legislation have perpetuated the lie that there is no need for such a bill—claiming that there is no law that challenges the freedom of speech of our churches. That propaganda is a blatant miscommunication of reality.

- The truth is simple: pastors, priests, rabbis, and clerics are forbidden to speak out on any topic that could be deemed "politically partisan." The IRS has even gone so far as to issue "code words" to tip it off to illegal activity. Words such as "pro-choice," "pro-life," "liberal," and "conservative" uttered from a pulpit, **even in an educationally motivated speech,** can warrant an investigation by the IRS.

- Even beyond the infringement on free speech, the current law is unconstitutional merely by the fact that it is unequally enforced. Day after day, Democrats make headlines standing in the pulpits of America's churches. Ironically, the IRS rarely opens an investigation to such clear-cut violations of the law in the more liberal churches. Instead, the conservative churches are the ones intimidated into silence.

- To have allowed the IRS to stand in judgment over our men and women of the cloth for the last fifty years is incomprehensible! First Amendment rights clearly state, "Congress shall make no law respecting an establishment of religion, or prohibiting the free exercise thereof; or abridging the freedom of speech." If we believe in the constitutional rights of our religious leaders, then **we must come together and support HR 235**.

- HR 235 boasts 165 cosponsors, both Democrats and Republicans. More than two dozen groups from all walks of faith have also submitted their written endorsement of this essential legislation.

Common Questions

Why was Freedom of Speech removed from houses of worship in the first place?

Today pastors do not have freedom of speech from behind the pulpit. The current law in the form of an IRS code is the cause of this lack of freedom. This law was inserted into the tax code by Senator Lyndon Johnson in 1954. Until that time, there were no restrictions on the church's role in politics. Although it probably was not "intended to target houses of worship," the law was intended to restrict organizations that opposed Johnson's reelection to the Senate. The reasons for this ban were never properly debated or voted on as a separate issue.

Will this mean that all sermons will be politically motivated?

Simply put, your pastor, priest, rabbi, or other religious leader here in America has the freedom to preach any message that he or she desires—with one exception. If your religious leader expresses an opinion, or makes a statement that is considered to "influence legislation" or "participate in, or intervene in (including the publishing or distributing of statements), any political campaign on behalf of (or in opposition to) any candidate for public office," he or she risks losing the tax-exempt status of the organization.

What religious denominations does this legislation affect?

All religions. All faiths support the Freedom of Speech Restoration Act. Why wouldn't they? Some churches and denominations currently speak freely from the pulpit about political issues, either because of their tax status or because their current political connections secure their 501(c)(3) status. HR 235 levels the playing field. All faith-based ministries will be free to speak their minds about any issues, including political or moral issues, without financial repercussion. This was the original intent of the framers of our Constitution. Since 1954, that right has been distorted, misused, and abused. This legislation simply corrects that injustice and levels the playing field for all faiths, religions, and denominations.

Is this legislation motivated by a particular faith or political party?

It is supported by all Americans across all faiths, regardless of their political or religious affiliations. It simply restores the First Amendment rights of all religious leaders to express their opinions to their congregations without the fear of revoking your place of worship's tax-exempt status.

CHAPTER 6

Making a Difference

Learn How To Communicate With Your Elected Officials In Ways That Get Results!

Napoleon Bonaparte once said, "There are only two powers in the world, the sword and the pens; and in the end the former is always conquered by the latter." Napoleon's axiom is well known. But in today's high-tech world, does it still ring true?

The editors of *Life* magazine think so. In the publication's September 29, 1997, issue they named the printing of the Gutenberg Bible in 1455 as the most important event of the last 1,000 years because it ushered in the information revolution.

TAKE UP YOUR...PENS!

The written word has always been a powerful tool, and thanks to a host of constitutionally protected freedoms, the power of the pen is even more potent in America today. Our nation's Constitution guarantees "freedom of speech, or of the press; or the right of the people peaceably to assemble and to *petition the government for a redress of grievances."* While freedom of speech and press gets lots of attention, the right to petition the government is also a fundamental freedom.

Since God's providence has granted America these freedoms, Christian citizens have a responsibility to exercise their rights wisely. That means answering the call to "take up your pens" (or your keyboard) and communicate with elected officials, or planning a visit to speak with a representative—all without fear of reprisal or punishment.

TAKING THAT FIRST STEP

It can seem intimidating at first to contact elected officials, but there are many ways available for citizens to let their voice be heard.

For example, grass roots organizations often conduct mass media campaigns designed to rally their constituents to action. These campaigns often take the form of petitions, postcards or telegrams. While such mass-produced petitions are less effective than personal correspondence, remember that most elected officials tally every constituent communication that comes to the office. Getting the attention of elected officials is often a numbers game.

Most representatives personally read only a small sampling of the mail from constituents. The volume is just too much. Therefore a system is in place that responds to letters.

The mail goes to a low-ranking staff member. He figures out your issue, tallies your response, and sends back one of several form letters that addresses your inquiries. If your letter is general in nature, you will get a generic, printed letter in return.

LET'S GET PERSONAL

Bruce Barron, former congressional aide, offers some

practical tips in his book, *Politics for the People,* to help concerned citizens get their views heard in the hallowed halls of our city, state and federal capitals.

How do you get past the standard response? According to Barron, "A personal phone call or, better yet, a concise, individually written letter will carry more weight."

The key is to write letters that stand out—letters that are different, letters that demand a personal response. That kind of letter gets noticed and draws attention to your cause. Here are a few reasons why:

1. A personal letter shows that you care about the issue.
2. A personal letter demonstrates that you act independently.
3. A personal letter says you are willing to invest time to get an answer.

INCREASING YOUR IMPACT

Here are a few tips to help your letter make an even greater impact.

1. **Ask very specific questions**. Make it your goal to ask questions so specific your elected official's staff cannot respond with a form letter. That forces the staff to provide clear answers.
2. **Offer a policy option**. Don't just express your disapproval or opposition; always list an alternative. Then ask the representative to address the implication of your alternate policy.
3. **Know the legislative process**. If you are vague about what they are doing, they can be vague in answering you. But if you ask your legislator to take specific action, he can't dodge your questions so easily.

4. **Keep up the dialogue**. If you get a response you don't like, call the congressman's district or federal office and politely but firmly ask for a complete answer.

This approach means you must "know your stuff" on the issue. You must be able to present it well and also be able to discern the elected official's response.

WOULD YOU HELP ME?

Another way of gaining a better audience to express your views is to get to know the staff member responsible for articulating the policy position for the elected official. Barron notes, "This approach is especially useful if you expect to communicate frequently on bills within a specific legislative area, such as education."

Though they have busy schedules, they often will be able to take the time to help you understand where a congressman stands on the issue in questions. Plus, they may help you find persuasive arguments.

PRACTICAL TIPS FOR EFFECTIVE LETTERS

1. **State your purpose right up front**. State it in the first paragraph of the letter. If your letter pertains to a specific piece of legislation, identify it appropriately. (House bill — H.R. _____/Senate bill — S._____)

2. **Always be courteous**. The Bible tells us to respect others because all men are made in the image of god, but also that we should "be in subjection to the governing authorities. For there is no authority except from God, and those which exist are established by God" (Romans 13:1).

3. **Address only one issue**. Avoid the temptation of

using a "shotgun" approach with a letter that tackles your hot-button issues. Instead, stay focused on one particular issue with each letter.

4. **Keep your letter to one page.** This is very important. A one-page letter speaks volumes to your ability to concisely and professionally communicate. If you need help keeping your letter to one page, ask a friend to edit it.

PLEASE SIT DOWN!

Of course, better than a letter or phone call to your elected official's office, you may want to make a personal visit. Every effort is made by the congressional staff to schedule meetings with constituents. That is a very effective way for you to convey a message about specific legislation.

To make the most of your personal visit with your elected official, here are some suggestions:

Plan your visit carefully. Be clear about your objectives. Know who you are going to meet with.

Make an appointment with the person in charge of the office schedule. This will help you get in touch with the right person so your issues are dealt with appropriately.

Be prompt and patient. It is not uncommon, due to last-minute changes in schedule, for a legislator to be late or have a meeting interrupted. But you can show your seriousness and professional attitude by being there on time. Of course, be flexible if interruptions do occur. By being on time, you can be ready to meet when the opportunity is open.

Like the Boy Scout handbook states—be prepared! Have your information and materials ready to support your position. Have copies ready for the official or his or her staff. If they are not aware of the details, your information may help them understand your position.

Be political. Since elected officials first and foremost want to represent their constituents in their district or state, show how your issue connects with them. Show how you can assist in communicating this information to his constituents.

Be responsive. Answer any and all questions—and always be candid with your response. Elected officials take seriously what their constituents say. Remember, to your elected official you represent the views of hundreds or perhaps thousands of people. But always speak your mind, not the opinion of "John Q. Public."

Follow up your meeting with a "thank you" letter. It is also appropriate to summarize the meeting and its main points. Include with your letter any additional information your elected official may have requested.

Communicating with elected officials is an important civic duty that can result in real changes that impact your community. So get started today!

Inform And Activate Your own pro-Family Network Without Leaving Your Home!

A few years back, legislation was introduced in the U.S. House of Representatives that threatened to give the government more control over private and home education in this nation. Several Christian and policy groups saw that this bill could have a devastating impact and began a nationwide effort to contact people who would be adversely effected.

From national offices, calls were made to state leaders who passed information to local offices. Within hours, phone chains and fax and e-mail networks were activated.

The reaction was immediate and overwhelming. Soon, elected officials at all levels of government were hearing from constituents voicing their concern. Phones rang off the hook. Fax machines printed out messages. Letters poured in by the thousands.

Legislators realized how their constituents wanted them

to vote on this issue, and the measure was defeated.

"THE BRITS ARE COMING!"

The concept of the grassroots information networks is not new. Think about the early days of the American Revolution. At a crucial time, Paul Revere received a message about enemy troops and quickly passed that information on to neighboring communities.

Paul Revere was part of a communications network. While seemingly primitive by our standards, the goals behind Revere's actions were the same goals that encompass a grassroots information network today:

1. informing people about controversial issues in a timely manner;
2. motivating your friends and neighbors to take action;
3. mobilizing people to respond quickly on critical issues;
4. unifying independent groups on issues of common concern;
5. creating opportunities for practical involvement in current issues.

These goals encompass the essence of grassroots activity. While they may seem lofty, these goals are easier to attain now than ever before!

YOU CAN DO IT TOO!

Like Paul Revere, you can effectively rally citizens to respond during a time of crisis through a phone/fax/e-mail network.

Such an information network provides a simple vehicle for making an immediate impact. And it is the key to winning most battles—especially those that require mobilizing support at the grassroots level in a very short time frame.

And best of all, a phone/fax/e-mail network requires minimal commitment from those involved. People can take part at little or no cost and without expending a lot of energy or time.

Remember, if each church member, coalition member, or neighborhood leader would do one thing a week—vote, write/call about an issue, visit an elected official, etc.—that would be over 50 actions a year! That makes a difference!

HOME BASED ACTIVISM

Another aspect of information networks that makes them so doable is that you never have to leave your home to make an impact! You don't have to ride around the neighborhood on a horse like Paul Revere, yelling the news in the middle of the night. With cellular phones, computers, and fax machines, it is easier than ever and can cost very little to gather and share information.

But don't think everything has to be "high-tech" to be effective. Sometimes simpler is better.

Often people get so enamored with the "gadgets" that they forget to remember the purpose of a network—getting the right information to the right people in a timely manner so action can be taken.

HOW TO GET STARTED

Where should you begin when building a grassroots information network? You only need three things: a network, a medium, and a message.

Launching your network. Getting your networks started is as easy as opening your personal address book. Friends and family are a great place to start. Your network may be made up of individuals in a small Bible study group or the members of a Sunday school class. The network can be extended to other groups as well.

Finding the right medium. Next, you need a medium. Since most people have a phone, start there with a simple telephone chain. The leader starts the message by calling three or four others. They in turn call three or four others. Fax machines create excellent citizenship networks (see guidelines below). If you have access to e-mail, a similar system can be set up between individuals by sending information via the Internet. This has the advantage of going right to a person's desk rather than sitting on a fax machine.

Setting guidelines. No matter which medium (or media) you choose, be sure the lines of communications are clearly defined:

1. Who is responsible for contacting whom and in what time frame?
2. What happens when someone can't be contacted?
3. Who determines what items are passed on?

FAX NETWORK TIPS

Here are some specific tips to help you launch an effective fax network:

1. The leader should have a fax machine that can store programmable phone numbers.
2. Interested activists should be encouraged to get a fax machine or set up fax software on their computers.
3. Program your fax or computer fax to make fax calls at night, thus avoiding peak business hours and saving you time sitting in front of a fax machine.
4. Fax clear copies—preferably originals.
5. Fax on a regular schedule (weekly) unless there is an urgent issue.
6. Limit faxes to two pages.

7. Only the fax leader should distribute faxes to the entire network.
8. Divide your list into two groups: direct fax lines and shared phone lines. Shared phone lines must be called prior to sending the fax.

There is one important tip for e-mail networks: Use the "bcc"/"blind carbon copy" feature when you send the e-mails, so your members names and e-mail addresses will not be revealed and their privacy will be protected.

WIDENING YOUR CIRCLE

If you want to reach beyond your own circle of friends or organization, these are some simple steps you can take.

Identify like-minded groups. Open up the Yellow Pages and begin calling churches and other groups that may share your concerns on issues such as education, crime, right-to-life, taxes, pornography, homosexuality, and parental rights. Ask to speak to the pastor or spokesperson. Tell him or her what you are doing and ask if he or she would like to be a part of your network.

Become a good networker. Whenever you are at a gathering, be quick to identify people who may be interested in your network. Carry a sample of your latest communication. Swap business cards and offer to include them in your network.

Other guidelines. As you build your list, remember these points:

a. Be sure to get correct spellings of all names of contact people.
b. Ask for fax numbers and e-mail addresses right away.
c. Provide a phone number for feedback and/or phone/address changes

FINAL POINTERS

No matter what form of communication your network takes on, it is critical to establish a few guidelines:

1. **Clarify the goal of each communication.** What do you want people to accomplish? If you are asking people to pray, say so. If you want them to take action—such as write a letter or call a politician—make the request clear. And be sure all information (phone numbers and/or addresses) is double-checked before releasing it on the network. Proper documentation assures that your information is accurate and gives credibility to your fax network.
2. **Keep each news item simple and direct.** Complicated items get garbled. People will be more likely to relay the message immediately if it only takes a moment. Simple requests always get a better response than complicated ones.
3. **If appropriate, list a phone number or address where more information can be obtained.** People with a greater interest in any topic may want to do more, and by directing them, you further the cause.
4. **Send the phone numbers/addresses/e-mails of elected officials, Congress, the White House, etc., *each time* you request that your network take action.**

READY, SET, GROW!

Remember—phone/fax/e-mail chains are almost organic in their nature. How they develop and evolve is beyond anyone's control. Your network will always be changing, so do not be disheartened if there are seasons where the network loses members. As issues come and go, your network will grow accordingly, and like the watchmen posted on the wall in biblical times and Paul Revere in our own nation's history, you can play a key role in alerting others to critical issues.

Contact the CENTER FOR RECLAIMING AMERICA for more information about how to establish your own network.

About the Author

Pastor, politician, activist, and musician, Gary Cass, D.Min., has entered the next phase of a life dedicated to serving our Lord Jesus Christ, as the Executive Director of the CENTER FOR RECLAIMING AMERICA. Gary came to Fort Lauderdale via San Diego, where for twenty years he served as a pastor — most recently at West Hills Christian Fellowship, a non-denominational church.

As a high school student, Gary was voted his school's "most talented" graduate, primarily for his virtuoso-like mastery of the saxophone. After a near fatal car accident in 1977, Gary met his Lord and Savior, who called him to use that musical gift to bring the Gospel to the world. As music director for Living Sound International (1979-1981), Gary took the Gospel behind the Iron Curtain at the height of the Cold War.

Gary's pastoral career began in 1981, as he assisted his father-in-law, the Reverend Jerry Barnard, at Christian Faith Centre in San Diego. Gary's intense study of the Scriptures began at this time, and, upon graduation from Vanguard University, he became a youth pastor and subsequently the senior associate minister of Christian Faith Centre.

Gary has definitively taken his faith into the public square, heeding the biblical call to be "salt and light" in the world. He is a tireless Christian warrior for God and has been an entrenched pro-life activist for many years. A spearhead of pro-life efforts in San Diego, Gary sponsored numerous pro-life rallies and worked diligently (and successfully) to shut down abortion clinics in the San Diego-area. In 2002, Gary received the California Life Coalition's Pro-Life Service Award for demonstrated excellence in his commitment to protecting life.

Not content with the status quo, Gary successfully ran for the Grossmont Union High School Board in 1998 and ended up the lone Christian of the board's five members. Through networking with other like-minded pastors, activists, and community members, Gary helped to change the composition of the school board. Upon his departure, after two-terms of service, four of the five members were Christian, showcasing Gary's impressive success rate when recruiting and running Christians for public office.

His broad political involvement also includes intense advocacy for Proposition 22, the measure passed by California voters in 2000 to protect traditional marriage.

Gary has been featured on Southern California's most listened to radio talks shows; the Roger Hedgecock Show, Crosstalk with Rich Agazino, and the Mark Larsen Show, and has been quoted in Christianity Today, World Magazine, and on Salem Radio Network News.

Gary holds a BA in biblical Studies from Vanguard University, an MA in Theology, and a D.Min (Preaching), from Westminster Theological Seminary in California.

Gary and Sandy, his wife of 23 years, have three children: Isaac, Joshua, and Sharaya, all of whom are active in Christian ministry.

Make a Difference Today!

Call and ask Congress to return Freedom of Speech to America's churches by passing the language in House Resolution 235. If you don't know who your Congressman is, please visit http://www.house.gov/writerep.

The House of Representatives
202-224-3121

Ways and Means Chairman, Bill Thomas
202-225-3625

The Speaker of the House, Dennis Hastert
202-225-0600

The House Majority Leader, Tom Delay
202-225-4000

Center for Reclaiming America

P.O. Box 632
Ft. Lauderdale, FL 33302
877-SALT-USA (725-8872)
www.ReclaimAmerica.org

127